No.1 2019

The Kenya SOCIALIST

Classes & Class Struggle in Kenya

The Origin and Meaning of the Name Mau Mau

The Ukombozi Library

Information as a tool of Liberation

Uni.Way House, Second Floor, University Way
Next to Lilian Towers Hotel
P.O. Box 62501-00200
Nairobi
Kenya
info.vitabkske@gmail.com
http://vitabooks.co.uk

The Kenya Socialist is published by Vita Books, Nairobi, Kenya.
Editors: Shiraz Durrani and Kimani Waweru
September 2019

The Kenya Socialist aims to encourage free flow of information, knowledge and discussion which can lead to a better understanding of socialism. It will seek to:

- Promote socialist ideas, experiences and world outlook
- Increase awareness of classes, class contradictions and class struggles in Kenya, both historical and current
- Expose the damage done by capitalism and imperialism in Kenya and Africa
- Offer solidarity to working class, peasants and other working people and communities in their struggles for equality and justice
- Promote internationalism and work in solidarity with people in Africa and around the world in their resistance to imperialism
- Make explicit the politics of information and communication as tools of repression and also of resistance in Kenya

The Kenya Socialist welcomes submission of relevant articles (normally up to 5,000 words) - send to The Editors at info.vitabkske@gmail.com. The submissions will be reviewed and the Editors reserve the right not to publish.

Vita Books or Editors do not necessary agree with the views of contributors.
The Kenya Socialist is available at: http://vitabooks.co.uk/the-kenya-socialist/

Paper copies are available from African Books
Collective (ABC) orders@africanbookscollective.com

ISBN 978-9966-133-81-6

Design & Layout: Kariuki Maina.
petermaina1st@gmail.com
+254 719 510 999

CONTENTS

EDITORIAL: Socialism is the way ahead

Kenya was a victim of colonialism for decades before armed resistance by people brought independence. Hopes were high then that the aims of resistance would be met: stolen lands would be returned to their rightful owners and a democratic, socialist state in which the people have the rights to be free from economic exploitation and social inequality would be established. But imperialism had other ideas. It was not going to let a rich economic and strategic country out of its grips. Small impediments such as independence do not come in the way of imperialist desire for profits and power.

One of the weapons imperialism used to retain control over Kenya — and other parts of Africa and the world — was capitalism which it had introduced right from the early days of colonial plunder. With its sharp class divisions, capitalism created an elite comprador class which was the natural ally of corporations and the ruling classes in imperialist countries. Bribing the Kenyan elite with other people's land, state power and all that goes with it was easily done as part of the independence package. There remained the small matter of the working class, the peasants, the poor, the landless and the unemployed who were necessary to capitalism in order to ensure that wealth continued to be produced to feed the imperialist-friendly elite and, of course, the corporations which supported them. But it was the workers and peasants who resisted imperialism, as they did colonialism. Imperialism then controlled this resistance through tough 'law and order' measures. When that failed to subdue them, the police, GSU, and the military trained by imperialism were ready to deal with 'dissidents', 'terrorists' and 'communists'. The new rulers turned Kenya into a prison without walls for the working people.

The people of Kenya did not choose capitalism, capitalism chose them as its victims. Having enslaved African people for centuries, capitalism changed tactics in the face of people's resistance. It unleashed the 'free' market forces to continue its exploitation. People had chosen socialism 'in light of the demonstrable superiority of socialist over capitalist methods in the task of overcoming the legacy of centuries of colonial oppression and to build a society free from exploitation' as Dubula (1965, 24) observed. Africanus (1963, 53) added, 'Africans have seen and suffered from capitalism at work in their midst, with its ruthless exploitation of human labour, its criminal disregard of the welfare, lives, health and interests of the people'. Kwena (1962) reinforces the message of the failure of capitalism:

A system based on private ownership of the means of production and whose sole purpose is to make profit, capitalism and its variants — colonialism, imperialism and fascism — has miserably failed to satisfy the needs of the mass of humanity … This is the case not only with regard to Africa, Asia and Latin America but everywhere where the system obtains.

But colonialism and neo-colonialism saw the danger that socialism posed to its freedom to loot, pillage and massacre and took steps to silence the message of socialism, in the process murdering, 'disappearing' and rendering powerless the leaders who stood for socialism: Pio Gama Pinto and Karimi Nduthu, to name just two. But the voice of socialism never died, it remained just below the surface and comes up every now and then. The Kenya Socialist is one such voice that stands with working people in their demand for equality, justice and freedom from exploitation and oppression which is possible only under socialism.

The Kenya Socialist will promote socialist ideas and socialist world outlook as a challenge to those of capitalism and imperialism that dominate Kenya's and Africa's mass media, education and government policies. It will provide the missing socialist perspective on issues of national interest. It is not neutral and is committed to supporting people's resistance to capitalism and imperialism whose ideology has been made the prevailing force since independence, while the voice of socialism has been systematically and forcefully silenced.

The starting point for The Kenya Socialist is Lenin:

We want to achieve a new and better order of society: in this new and better society there must be neither rich nor poor; all will have to work. Not a handful of rich people, but all the working people must enjoy the fruits of their common labour. Machines and other improvements must serve to ease the work of all and not to enable a few to grow rich at the expense of millions and tens of millions of people. This new and better society is called socialist society - (Lenin's Collected Works, Vol 6, p.366).

This matches with the aims of Kenya's war of

independence, as summed up by Pio Gama Pinto:

Kenya's Uhuru must not be transformed into freedom to exploit, or freedom to be hungry, and live in ignorance. Uhuru must be Uhuru for the masses — Uhuru from exploitation, from ignorance, disease and poverty.

The sacrifices of the hundreds of thousands of Kenya's freedom fighters must be honoured by the effective implementation of KANU's policy —a democratic, African, socialist state in which the people have the rights, in the words of the KANU election manifesto, "to be free from economic exploitation and social inequality" Pio Gama Pinto (1963): Glimpses of Kenya's Nationalist Struggle.Pan Africa, Kenya Uhuru Souvenir issue, 12-12 1963.

The Kenya Socialist will:

• Promote socialist ideas, experiences and world outlook
• Increase awareness of classes, class contradictions and class struggles in Kenya, both historical and current
• Expose the damage done by capitalism and imperialism in Kenya and Africa
• Offer solidarity to working class, peasants and other working people and communities in their struggles for equality and justice
• Promote internationalism and work in solidarity with people in Africa and around the world in their resistance to imperialism
• Make explicit the politics of information and communication as tools of repression and also of resistance in Kenya

The Kenya Socialist does not stop at making theoretical and historical material available to readers. An equally important task is the one it shares with Vita Books and the Ukombozi Library: connecting and working with communities and peoples. It is an activist journal and hopes to work with, and for, the marginalised and oppressed people through their trade unions and social or community organisations.

This first issue covers several areas that remain neglected in public discourse in Kenya. The study of class remains one such topic and Kimani Waweru's article, Class and Class Struggle in Kenya, fills this gap.Waweru also contributes a briefing on ideology as a weapon of oppression or liberation.

He will continue his theoretical explorations in the next issue with an article on gender and women's oppression and liberation.

History is never far from any liberation struggle. Nicholas Mwangi looks at Mau Mau and the origin and meaning of the term 'Mau Mau'.

Njoki Wamai's contribution is her presentation at the All African Peoples' Conference in Accra in 2018. Wamai documents the pioneering Ukombozi Library established in Nairobi by the Progressive African Library & Information Activists' Group (PALIAct) in partnership with Vita Books and Mau Mau Research Centre as a 'library to liberate minds' and highlights the needs for relevant information in people's struggle for liberation.

Linking up with the launch of the Ukombozi Library, the question arises, 'What is the role of information in liberation?' Shiraz Durrani answers some question from Julian Jaravata on various aspects of information.

Finally, Durrani looks at the challenge by Wakamba wood carvers to the information embargo under President Moi.

References

Africanus, Terence (1963): A Note on Mr. Mboya's 'Socialism'. South African History Online. Marxist- Leninist Study. https://www.sahistory.org.za/.../Acv2n463.0001.9976.002.004.1963.9.pdf [Accessed: 26- 05-9].

Dubula, Sam (1965): A Socialist Label for Bourgeois Thinking. South African Communist Party. Available at:https://www.sahistory.org.za/sites/default/files/DC/Acn2265.0001.9978.000.022.1965.5/Acn2265.0001.9978.000.022.1965.5.pdf. [Accessed: 25-05-19].

Kwena, Jalang (1962): National Independence & Socialism: A continent in search of a formula. South African History Online. Available at: https://www.sahistory.org.za/sites/default/files/DC/Acn1062.0001.9976.000.010.Jul1962.7/Acn1062.0001 .9976.000.010.Jul1962.7.pdf [accessed: 27-05-19].

by Shiraz Durrani
Kimani Waweru

CLASSES AND CLASS STRUGGLE IN KENYA

by Kimani Waweru

Class can be said to be the differences of people position in the system of social production. A group of people within a society who are in a particular position belongs to the same class e.g. producers in a capitalist country are the working class while those who control and direct the process of production are the capitalist class. The division of society into classes means that one class is exploiting the labour of another and therefore expropriating the social surplus created by the productive class. The relations between the exploiting and exploited classes are antagonistic because workers (producers) want their wages to be increased while the capitalists (owners of means of production) want to reduce wages so that they can increase their profits. This is why the capitalist system is full of irreconcilable contradictions that can only be resolved by revolution. The dominant class that appropriates social wealth in terms of profit also controls ideas of the society and believes those ideas are in the interests of the society and humanity in general. It is no wonder that the ruling ideas, as Marx said, are those of the ruling class.

The emergence of class division is related to the advancement of productive forces and consequently the emergence of private property. The ruling class tends to show that classes are eternal but this has been proven to be wishful thinking by the principles of social science as we will see. Social science helps us to understand that classes emerged when society reached a certain stage of development. This fact is proven to be true by recent scientific findings of people whose development stage lagged behind the rest e.g. Iroquois Native Americans who lived in a classless society before the invasion of their land by foreigners in the 14th century. In Africa, San people of Bostwana were living in a primitive communal society (hunters and gatherers) with no classes some few decades ago. The advancement of productive forces (labour and instruments of labour) over thousands of years led to emergence of one mode of production after the other, the latter being higher than the one preceding it. In the European society which is widely documented, we find that the four modes of production have evolved i.e. primitive communalism, slavery, feudal and now capitalism. Each mode of production, apart from primitive communalism, had classes e.g. slaves and slave owners under slavery, lords and serfs under feudalism and capitalists and workers under capitalism. This therefore means the appropriation

of social wealth by the minority was not only in the capitalist system but also in other modes of production that preceded capitalism.

There are a number of people especially in Africa who dismiss the idea of development of classes as mentioned in the above paragraph. They claim the idea is European and lack any relevance to Africa; some raise the issue genuinely while others happen to be agents of the status quo who love to poison any idea that threatens the status quo. This situation is aggravated by the fact that African history is not much documented and most of what was documented was destroyed by foreigners who conquered the African territories. For example when Portuguese conquered Mombasa, they destroyed the city together with the artifacts. In Kenya it is sometimes a challenge to get history from the 14th, 15th and 16th centuries that shows how Kenyan nationalities used to live before the coming of foreigners. But one thing that is not in dispute is that the entrance of foreigners in the country upset the production processes and the social set up. Their forces of production were also affected, thus forcing most of the nationalities to adopt capitalism (capitalist relations imposed by colonialism through forcing peasants out of land, taxation, introduction of the kipande system etc.) When we apply scientific analysis method in analysing the Kenyan situation, we would not fail to understand that the same principles that were applied by the social scientists of past centuries from Europe and wherever else can also be used in the Kenyan situation. Science can be applied by common people in that it is a process of understanding and transforming material reality to correspond with objective reality. It requires proof and evidence that something exist i.e. It is an evidence-based process. It is totally different from mysticism that invokes imaginary things without providing actual evidence. Mysticism is loved by the ruling class as it makes masses ignorant of dynamism of nature and society. Science, as Neil deGrasse Tyson (an American astrophysicist) said, allows one to confront and identify problems, to recognize problems and figure out how to solve them, rather than run away from them. Failure to apply scientific principles, as Ardea Skybreak (an ecology and evolutionary biology scientist) said, will make one to be vulnerable to manipulation and not being able to tell what's right from what's wrong, what's true from what's false.[1] Another thing that needs to be understood about science is that it is universal, meaning that there cannot be a science for Europe, Africa, Asia or America. One cannot say that they will study chemistry of Africa and not of America because the principles of chemistry are the same. Likewise one cannot say there is social science for Europe and that for Africa, science is science. Therefore scientific analysis that have shown that classes are found in a society where there is private appropriation of social production, and in order to eliminate them one has to get rid of private property, can also be applied in Kenya. This again does not mean copy-pasting rather applying scientific principles according to concrete condition.

Classes in Kenya

Kenya can be termed as a neo-colonial country, meaning that it is subservient to the imperialist countries. All the neo-colonial countries adhere to capitalist mode of production and also give a leeway to imperialists to steal the resources. This is one of the reasons that most of the neo-colonial countries are underdeveloped and unable to meet the needs of their people. The foreign capital that the imperialists bring to Kenya, as Nkrumah said is used for exploitation rather than for development[2]. When the so-called investments under neo-colonialism increase, they [investments] widen the gap between the rich imperialists and the poor third world counties such as Kenya. Nkrumah, in few words, termed neo-colonialism as a representation of imperialism in its final and perhaps its most dangerous stage.

The neo-colonial countries have different types of classes and Kenya is not exceptional. Every class has its own attitude towards change in the society. This is contrary to what the ruling class preaches that all people share the same outlook or attitude. Class analysis is therefore very important for those who want to bring fundamental changes in Kenya; the changes that will help the majority to enjoy basic and other needs that make humans live a life of dignity.

Comprador Bourgeois

This is a class that is most dangerous in that it helps in promoting the imperialist agenda by siphoning national wealth and expropriating it to the former colonial masters. This class consists of the most senior people working and seating in the boards of multi-national companies in Kenya. The class also consists of the ruling political elite (leadership of Jubilee, CORD etc.) that promotes the same. Since independence the political class have been comprador. The said class rarely questions the

directive of the imperialists. For example during the 2007/8 general elections violence, the two main contenders (Kibaki and Raila) were directed by the imperialists to seat together and consequently form a coalition government. This was due to the fact that violence was affecting their (imperialists) investments and not that they were concerned about Kenyans killing one another. The class has allowed imperialist countries such as US and Britain to put their military bases in the country and who sometimes harass ordinary Kenyans with impunity. When the needs of the people collide with those of the imperialists, the comprador sides with those of imperialists. The comprador only supports the needs of the people when there is too much pressure or when an issue is so much exposed that ignoring it would expose the class for what it is. The political class cunningly pretends to be giving preference to the interests of the people while in actual fact prioritising those of imperialists. For example according to the media, during a Small and Medium-sized Enterprises (SMEs) Conference held at Strathmore University on 15th October 2018, President Uhuru Kenyatta trashed his written speech, saying the government has not improved conditions for small and medium enterprises. He lamented that the imported fish was strangling local fishermen and urged officials to find creative ways around the legal provisions, such as citing health concerns. This was after small scale traders, especially from the fisheries sector, complained of lack of protection from international players such as China who were exporting cheaper fishes thus killing local fish industries. The pressure from the traders forced the government to place a ban on Chinese fish. In retaliation China, which is now an imperialist country, acted the same way as other imperialists by threatening to impose trade sanctions against Kenya. Kenya being a comprador state chickened out and then tactfully lifted the fish ban ostensibly to allow for what it termed as consultations between Kenya and China.

The comprador class defends the status quo and cannot in any way support the people in bettering their living standards. It controls the state machineries which it uses to crush any resistance that may threaten its existence. It is therefore the target of revolution

National Bourgeois

National bourgeois are Kenyan people who have a substantial amount of wealth which they have invested and use to employ people. Members of this class include entities like Chris Kirubi, Manu Chandaria, S.K. Macharia, Naushad Merali, Moi family, Kenyatta family etc. These are people who are happy with the way things are since they are able to squeeze surplus labour from their workers without any hindrance. They have close ties with the system and always expend huge financial might to support the competing presidential candidates during the general elections so that their investments can be protected. They also align themselves to the system so they can get business contracts and licenses from the government. Many have immensely increased their wealth courtesy of their fanatic support to the neo-colonial government. In the 1990s for example, SK Macharia was one of the few Gikuyu elite who were supporting the KANU government under the banner "The Central Province Development Support Group."

In appreciation, the Moi regime readily issued him with a broadcasting license for his company Royal Media. The regime believed that being a staunch KANU supporter, he would use his radio station to support the government. This was not to be as he went the way of the quintessential capitalist. He was more focused on returns on his investment and thus opted to run his company professionally, giving both opposition and government enough airtime. This was meant to increase wider listenership and ultimately profits. The government was not pleased by his move and therefore closed Royal Media down for a couple of years, only to reopen after Macharia pleaded with President Moi. In the 2002 general elections, S.K. Macharia shifted his allegiance and used his station to vigorously campaign for the opposition (National Rainbow Coalition) and this contributed to the coalition's victory. Upon formation of the NARC government the station grew exponentially, getting government advertising contracts as well as being granted with several radio frequency licenses. As a result, Royal Media is the biggest electronic media house in Kenya today. This clearly shows that the national bourgeois class is usually propped up by the neo-colonial regime.

The national bourgeois class is against foreign investors as it sees them as competitors. Many times the class is therefore at the forefront preaching in support of protection of local companies (or nationalism) just to advance its selfish agenda. What matters to the members of this class is how they can increase profits. They do not really care about the suffering of the ordinary people whom they deem as a lazy lot condemned to their fate by their own bad choices. They ignorantly claim that the wealth they have amassed is as a result of their hardwork and not from the exploitation of the working class. They use the profits extracted from workers to fund charitable activities in a guise to hide their exploitative nature. They do these, as Susan Rosenthal said, to cleverly pose as social saints, shape society in their image and create confusion about the nature of capitalism.

The class also uses its financial muscles to influence peoples' thinking through their own media. Big media companies (Nation Group, Standard Group, Royal Media, Mediamax and Radio Africa) are owned by this class. The said media houses distort the truth and only tell the truth when it suit the capitalists. This class is hostile to any change that would bring fundamental changes, and always readily joins hands with the comprador class to fight the revolutionaries whenever the capitalist system is in danger. This therefore means that it is a target of revolution.

Peasants

They are mostly found in rural areas and mostly engage in agriculture. They are in two categories; the rich and the poor.

Rich Peasants

This category owns huge tracts of land that they use for subsistence as well as in commodity production (commercial).They employ temporary labourers whom they pay either daily, weekly or monthly. Rich peasants are the minority. Since they are driven by the urge to make a profit they exploit the labourers, majority whom are poor peasants who supplement their needs by selling their labour power. When it comes to the issue of change in the society, the rich peasants waver as they are usually afraid of fundamental changes that would cost them their status. Ironically, they are at the same time usually angry with the system for not subsidizing farm inputs such as fertilisers, seeds etc. This class is quite unpredictable, only rising up in protest when things are not working in their favour. As a result of this flaw, this class cannot be fully relied upon in bringing fundamental changes. The revolutionaries need to discern when the said class can be an ally and when it can be an impediment to the revolution.

Poor Peasants

Poor peasants are the majority. They have small parcels of land that they use for subsistence farming. Some also engage in zero grazing and sell their meagre products in markets or dairies. They are, however, in most times forced to supplement their subsistence needs by selling their labour power to rich peasants or other owners of means of production. They have groups such as merry-go-rounds through which they support themselves economically. They possess togetherness and assist one another in times of misfortune. They are religious and conservative. Some are organised into cooperative societies that market their produce to various parastatals bodies such as Kenya Tea Development Authority (KTDA), National Cereals and Produce Board (NCPB), Kenya Planters Cooperative Union (KPCU), Mumias Sugar etc. The parastatal entities normally buy the peasants' farm produce very cheaply, making it impossible for the peasants to solely rely on the said produce for livelihood. Some peasants have formed their own groups to fight against exploitation by the parastatal bodies. For example, tea farmers have Kenya Union of Small Scale Tea Owners (KUSSTO). KUSSTO has been spearheading advocacy for the rights of tea farmers for more than 10 years. Not surprisingly, this has often put the leadership of this organisation on a collision course with the authorities. More often than not this has led to their victimization and harrassment. The leaders are arrested and often suspended from delivering their tea produce to their respective tea factories. This harassment and intimidation is usually orchestrated and engineered by KTDA.In some instances the cooperative directors, who are normally elected by farmers to watch out for their interests, get financial favours from KTDA and thus remain silent as farmers get milked dry of their rightful dues. In many instances the peasants get fed up and rise in protest against this exploitation. In Kisii County for example, tea farmers at the

Itumbe tea factory, Sameta sub-county, held a protest on 17th April 2018 citing frustrations and poor management of the facilities by the top brass. Majority of members of cooperative societies are elderly people who in most cases tend to stick to old ways of doing things as opposed to young people who are normally more dynamic and aggressive. This challenge hinders them from agitating for their rights more robustly.

When it comes to change, poor peasants remain dormant and conservative even if they are being exploited. This makes it easy for them to be manipulated by the ruling class. The revolutionaries have to realise this so that they can know how to awaken them into fully joining the revolution. In early 20th century Lenin, in one of his speeches, said that peasants *"cannot immediately accept change because they cling firmly to what they are accustomed they are cautious about innovations subjects what they are offered to a factual practical test and does not decide to change their way of life until they are convinced that change is necessary"*. Therefore this is one thing that we should understand when dealing with the peasants so that they can be won over and partner with the workers in fighting for genuine change.

Mao Zedong did a scientific analysis of Chinese society and understood the weakness and strength of poor peasants. It is from this understanding that he was able to guide the Chinese masses,

Tea farmers in Nyamira protest ... on bonus pay in 201.. - Daily Nation

majority of whom were peasants, to victory in 1949. Poor peasants can be profoundly revolutionary when guided well and this means they are the key ally of the workers as well as revolutionaries.

Pastoralists

Pastoralism is largely associated with the culture traditions of some marginalized nationalities in Kenya. It is also associated with class because most of pastoralists practice pastoralism as a way of producing their livelihood. Pastoralist culture and livelihood is shaped by the livestock that they rear for meat, blood and milk. They are mostly found in remote areas, and particularly in the Northern part of Kenya where there is lack of infrastructure and basic services. They occupy more than 60% of total land in Kenya, although the larger part of this area is arid and semi-arid. The Maasai, Turkana, Pokot, Samburu and Rendille etc., are all pastoralists. Many pastoralist groups are very conservative as they have, for many years, rigidly stuck within traditional cultural practices and animal husbandry even when the practices have been overtaken by time and contextual changes. In recent times a small percentage have started to diversify by

cultivating various crops on small parcels of land. The money economy has forced some to exchange their animals for cash, thus deepening their incorporation within the market economy. In their urge to maximize their wealth some pastoralist groups engage in cattle rustling using sophisticated firearms, thus exacerbating insecurity in pastoral regions. This urge has caused them to go against cultural practices which forbade the killing of women and children during such the raids.

Most of the leaders from the region are, in most cases, anointed by ethnic spiritual leaders as the traditional norms dictate. This is one of the reasons the leaders are highly regarded by their respective communities and in most cases use this loyalty to manipulate their subjects into fighting neighbouring communities. The ruling class, knowing too well how influential these leaders are, normally wins them over and uses them to make the pastoralists ignorant of their predicament. The pastoralist class though, being one of the groups marginalized by the system, remain inactive and their anger to their predicament is, most times, triggered by their leaders cum politicians. Therefore this class happens to be a very unpredictable one to organize

with for the actual revolution.

Semi Proletariat (Traders, Petty Traders, Boda Boda Riders)

The Kenyan economy has, for a number of years, witnessed minimal growth and therefore is unable to absorb the thousands of youth who complete school every year. It is due to this that most people have opted to engage in small businesses in order to earn their livelihoods. The traders are exploited by the landlords, with their meager earnings mostly going to rent leaving them with almost nothing for their upkeep. Both National and county governments do not spare them, taxing them exorbitantly and also harassing them by detaining their imported wares. This has, in some instances, forced some to take to the streets in protest. In July 2018 for example, hundreds of traders poured into the streets of Nairobi in protest against harassment and intimidation by government agencies. They also complained of outrageous duty tax imposed by the Kenya Revenue Authority (KRA), exorbitant license fees among other issues.

Traders from Nairobi's Wakulima Market protesting increase of service fees by the Nairobi county government in 2014 – Daily Nation

The problem is that the said protests are mostly spontaneous and only aimed at short term goals. Since most of small scale traders live from hand to mouth, they are unable to prolong the protest for the actualisation of their demands. They also lack a strong organisation to spearhead and direct their struggle. This class can be an ally of the revolutionaries only when it is conscientised that their predicament is as a result of the capitalist system. A section of the class also aspires to be part of the bourgeoisis class.

The Proletariat or Working Class

The working class have potential of bringing fundamental change and are the engine to the revolution. This statement is not rhetoric, rather it is based on the fact that workers live on their labour power to survive since they do not have means of production (industries, equipment, materials, etc.) to produce what they need. They hold a powerful position in the dynamics of the capitalist system. Without them capitalism cannot function i.e. capitalists cannot survive without workers but workers can survive very well without capitalists. The workers are not a homogeneous there are skilled and unskilled. The unskilled are the most exploited and in most cases are forced to wake up early and walk to their places of work to save busfare. They also get home late, thus getting little time to bond with their children.

The working class in Kenya is not powerful and this could be attributed to the ineptitude of the Central Organisation of Trade Union (COTU) which is the umbrella body of all the private trade unions in Kenya. Since its establishment, COTU has always been on the side of the ruling class, though always disguising itself as a workers' advocate through issuing "progressive" rhetorical statements in public forums and in press conferences. Around Easter time in 1982, COTU failed to give leadership to workers who wanted to go on strike in solidarity with the workers of Bank of Baroda who had been dismissed. During the Structural Adjustment Programmes (SAPs) that were spearheaded by IMF, and led to the loss of many jobs, COTU didn't fight the said policies. In most cases the trade union officials fight for their stomachs, ignoring the workers they represent. To them workers are only important during the organisation's elections. They buy their votes during such elections and upon being elected embark on using their offices to solicit for bribes from the employers. For example, two officials of the Kenya County Government Workers Union (KCGWU) (Benson Olianga, the Nairobi City branch secretary, and John Muriuki, assistant treasurer) were arrested by anti-corruption detectives after they were caught soliciting a bribe from Governor Mike Sonko's aide in October 2017. The Kenyan trade unions lack working-class ideology that can assist them in combining advocacy for political and economic rights in a way similar to what Makhan Singh did in the 1940s and 50s, where he linked the workers' struggles with the political struggle for national liberation.

Though beset by the above challenges, Kenyan workers continue to resist oppression through protesting. On 31st October 2018 for example, workers from China Wuyi Precast Company situated in Athi River, Kajiado County, went on strike over

Mumias Sugar Company workers protesting delayed salary payment in street of Mumias town in September 2018 – The Standard

poor pay by the Chinese Company. When Kenyan workers today are dismissed by their employers, they unite in demanding for their dues. A case in point is when more than 600 former workers of the East African Portland Cement Company (EAPCC) protested on 14th October 2018 over their unpaid dues amounting to 1.5 billion shillings. The company had failed to pay them despite the court ruling.

These examples clearly show that the workers have great potential of bringing change in the country when led by a clear-sighted and disciplined organisation. The said organization helps in guiding workers to navigate through traps laid by the capitalists (employers) and leads them in waging the class war. The employers are very powerful as they are connected to the state and that why they use the state machinery, such as the police, to suppress protesting workers.

Workers are key ally of revolutionary change.

Petty Bourgeois

Petty bourgeois (middle class) in Kenya can be divided into three sections;

The Lower Petty Bourgeosis

They can be called the left wing of petty bourgeoisie as they are closer to workers and they are also victims of exploitation. This section consists of teachers, nurses etc. and is the most active of the three since it has strong organisations i.e. Kenya Union of Post Primary Education Teachers (KUPPET), Kenya National Union of Teachers (KNUT) and Kenya National Union of Nurses (KNUN). Their problem is that they rarely protest about issues affecting the country, the education or health sectors. Most of the time they protest due to salaries and allowance issues, and an example is the strike which the KNUT and KUPPET called in January 2015 (lasted three weeks) and September 2015 (lasted five weeks).

They are always indecisive as they keep on wavering and this is something that any revolutionary should understand. They can be at one time on the side of the workers or revolutionaries during hard times but on the side of the ruling class when their things are running well.

Teachers Protesting Over Poor Pay outside Parliament Buildings in September, 2011– Reuters

The Middle Petty Bourgeois

The middle petty bourgeois consists of doctors, engineers, professors and highly skilled people. They are bribed by the capitalists through being granted wages and privileges well beyond other workers, but do not have significant power. They live relatively well, which means that they have a vested interest in maintaining the status quo. They play very big role in capitalist economy due to their expertise in different fields. They are the main drivers in the neo-colonial Kenya as they are used to draft government policies. They rarely protest as conditions allow them to live comfortably, although in recent times the doctors have been up in arms protesting against the national government. However, their protests are opportunistic and not geared to helping the oppressed as they would like portray. For example in late 2016 and early 2017 doctors went on strike for a hundred days demanding the implementation of a Collective Bargaining Agreement (CBA) signed in 2013 which had awarded them 300 per cent pay hike. They had vowed to go on with the strike until their

pay demands were met.

But when the public started wondering why they were only focusing on their salaries they cunningly changed the tune and begun to address the rampant drug and equipment shortages, saying they were doing so for the sake of patients. Human rights activists working in NGO industry can be categorized in this class as their attitude towards change is similar. They abhor the abuses perpetrated by the regime and they are good at criticising the state and in articulating the problems and what need to be done. In addition, some go to an extent of saying that what is needed is revolution. On the other hand they are able to enjoy some privileges such as medical cover, a good salary and good housing under the current state of capitalism. And when it comes to the actual action they tend to shy away since they are not willing to forego the said privileges, since a revolution is not a joke; or as Mao said it is not "a dinner party, or writing an essay, or painting a picture, or doing embroidery", and it demands dedication and sacrifice that the

Doctors on Strike in 2017 - Daily Nation

humans rights activists are not prepared to give. There are a few people of this class who decide to forego the said privileges, rocking the boat and committing what Amilcar Cabral called class suicide by siding with the people in fighting for the real change. Most of the world revolutions in the world were led by such people e.g. Lenin in Russia, Cabral in Guinea Bissau and, Fidel Castro in Cuba etc. The revolutionaries can partner with the class when the state has turned fascist and curtailing democratic space i.e. in fighting for bourgeois democracy. Not many people of this class are usually ready to go beyond a bourgeois democracy i.e. to the actual revolution.

The Upper Petty Bourgeois

The upper petty bourgeois are the senior people of big local as well as national government. Their status helps them live comfortably since they get many benefits in terms of allowances. They always inspire to be national bourgeois and don't see

any problem with the capitalist system. They are indifferent towards the predicaments of the lower classes, and in most cases they view them with contempt. It would take a major economic crisis for this class to rise up against the government and join the revolutionaries.

Lumpen-proletariat

Lumpenproletariats mostly live in slums and are the most exploited and dehumanised by the system. The majority have limited levels of education and are unskilled. They include muggers, prostitutes, petty thieves and those who have stayed long without getting employed. This class mostly depend on the handouts of bourgeoisie on a day-to-day basis and will do anything in order to survive. This is why it is used by politicians to do all manner of dirty work including violently harassing and intimidating rivals. It is also used by NGOs to fulfil their project goals e.g. attending workshops. On the other hand some members of this class can become agents for change if they are made conscious about their predicament by people who have a clear and pro people ideology. The class shares the same characteristics as the petty bourgeois, in terms of political wavering, and cannot be the main force for change in Kenya.

Who are Friends and Enemies of Change in Kenya?

Science helps us not to take class attitudes as cast in stone. A few people belonging to a particular class may have a different attitude. In science there are usually abnormalities where classes don't always follow the rules. For example, majority of mammals give birth but there are some like the platypus that lay eggs. This should not negate the fact that mammals are associated with giving birth as opposed to laying eggs. The same applies to social sciences. The majority of people belonging to a particular class have a similar attitude to life but this is not true of the entire class. Science also helps us not to be rigid but open to all dimensions especially when tackling a complex matter. One thing that should be understood, as Ardea Skybreak said, is that there is no such thing as fixed and unchanging human nature or unchangeable human nature. The conception or outlook, though shaped by material reality, is also largely influenced by the ruling class whose ideas are the dominant ones or are dominant. But once the exploited, probably through a vanguard, are guided and grounded enough they begin to understand things better, changing their views and misconceptions and ultimately start organising on how they can bring change for the betterment of humanity.

The above class stratification, as well analysis shows us clearly that those who are the most exploited by the system are bound to yearn for change, while those who benefit from it will defend the status quo. Since no genuine change can come about without involving the people it is therefore important to reach them. The history of our country shows us that over the years people have failed to achieve what they want due to aligning themselves with the wrong people. For instance in the 1950s, the petty bourgeoisie within KAU had disguised themselves as advocates for the land and freedom struggle that was being waged by the Mau Mau. However behind the scenes they were busy courting and cavorting with colonialists and demonising the movement. The masses, who were not well advanced in political discernment, embraced them based on their dishonest politicking only to be disappointed after Kenya attained the 'flag independence'. Therefore, it is usually important to do a class analysis so that people can know the right people to align with, and not be deceived by words and superficial deeds.

In Kenya peasants, workers and the lower petty bourgeois remain the leading force for change, and what they need most is a progressive movement offering them leadership and ideology. With those two they can accomplish what might be seen as impossibilities and bring change that is beneficial to the majority.

The middle petty bourgeois waver between the oppressor and the oppressed, they only join the side of the oppressed when they are in problems. Therefore the people should be wary of them due to their opportunism.

National, international and comprador bourgeoisie are those we should aim to defeat since they own the means of production and they use it to exploit workers and strongly defend the status quo. They are the most powerful force as they control the state machinery. Revolutionary changes which have occurred in the world have shown that even with the power they possess, these classes are usually defeated by organised masses led by a revolutionary party.

Further Reading

Kinyattiĩ M., 2008, Classes and Class Struggle in Kenya, Mau Mau Research Centre, Nairobi

Lenin V.L., 1917, A Class Shift, Lenin Collected Works, Vol. 25, First published in Pravda No. 92, July 10 (June 27), Moscow

Marx K. & Engels F., Manifesto of the Communist Party, Foreign Languages Publishing House, Moscow, 1893

Mathema N.C.G., 1987, The Philosophy of the Working Class, Memorial Co-operative Society Limited, Harare

Tse Tung M., 1971, Analysis of the Classes in Chinese Society – Selected Readings from the Work of Mao Tse Tung

End Notes

1. Science and Revolution - An Interview with Ardea Skybreak 2015

2. Nkrumah K, 1965, Neocolonialism: the Last Stage of Imperialism, Thomas Nelson & Sons Ltd., London

"In the mouths of the Government and K.A.N.U. leaders, African socialism has become a meaningless phrase. What they call African socialism is neither African nor socialism. It is a cloak for the practice of total capitalism. To describe the policies of the present government as African socialism is an insult to the intelligence of people. The deception is obvious but the leaders of the Government and of K.A.N.U. do not have the courage to admit that they are fully committed to the Western ideology of capitalism." - KPU Manifesto, 1966.

ORIGIN AND THE MEANING OF THE NAME MAU MAU
by Nicholas Mwangi

The struggle in Kenya by the Mau Mau movement [1948-1960) is a revolutionary chapter in the history of Kenya and revolutions in the South. It is this revolution, under the leadership of Field Marshall Dedan Kimathi, that won Kenya its freedom from British colonialism. It used tactics of guerilla warfare as a way to achieve independence and end colonialism in Kenya. The Mau Mau movement has commanded the attention of researchers and scholars on the subject of revolutionary uprising and rebellion for years, with every scholar giving their own perspectives of the Mau Mau struggle.

Mau Mau war was fought by the peasants, working class, landless squatters and the urban poor, with the trade unions forming the backbone of the organization. The trade unions led by Makhan Singh, Chege wa Kibacia, Fred Kubai and Bildad Kaggia were key in organizing workers, who would later formed the militant forces of Mau Mau. It is the trade unions that provided Mau Mau with a revolutionary agenda. It was the only revolutionary movement in Africa that did not receive any military assistance in terms of weapons or training from the outside world, compared to other movements such as African Independence Party for Guinea and Cape Verde's (PAIGC) guerilla movement in Guinea, the Mozambique Liberation Front (FRELIMO) in Mozambique or the Peoples Movement for the Liberation of Angola (MPLA). Mau Mau organized its fighting forces in small battalions, used stolen or self-made weapons and united its forces by a loyalty oath. It thus launched one of the most dramatic and revolutionary wars of its time against the British Empire.

The movement developed out of the radical quarters of Kenya African Union led by Fred Kubai and Bildad Kaggia, both from the radical trade union movement who had come to believe that the British would not give Kenya its independence through negotiations.

Though Mau Mau has continued to be an interesting topic for researchers, historians and the general public, it also seems to be a mystery to many, especially in regard to its origins. One aspect that lacks clarity is the origin and meaning of the name Mau Mau. This article examines the origin and meaning of the term Mau Mau as argued by various scholars and as interpreted in various documents.

General Mwariama and Mau Mau Guerrila Army in 1964

The most popular version of the origin of the name is the claim that Mau Mau was the acronym for the Kiswahili phrase *Mzungu Aende Ulaya- Mwafrika Apate Uhuru* (Let the white man go back to Europe so that the African can become Independent).
The surviving Mau Mau freedom fighters have disagreed on this version. According to Bildad Kaggia (Kaggia, B., Leeuw and M. Kaggia 2012), a member of the Central Committee, Mau Mau has no meaning in either Kikuyu or Kiswahili.

The name Mau Mau has also been associated with the numerous mountains bordering the Rift-Valley, North-East of lake Naivasha, from where Mau Mau activities were believed to have sought and obtained inspiration and guidance in their revolt against imperial rule (Alau, Abiodun 2006,pg 5)

J.M Kariuki (1975, p 24) Give's a detailed account of how the name Mau Mau might have originated:

One evening, people went to a house in Naivasha area where the oath was to be administered. It was the duty of the administrator to see that there was a reliable guard to keep watch outside while the oath was being administered. That evening, the guard was given instructions that should he hear any footsteps and suspected it was the police or the enemy, he should shout the anagram 'Mau Mau 'so that those in the house couldW escape. It would be a clear sign only for those in the house, for the enemy would not understand what the words 'Mau Mau 'meant. That night the police did come to the house and the guard shouted out. The people left the house. When the police came they found no people but the oathing paraphernalia only. When they reported back to the police headquarters, they said they heard the words 'Mau Mau' being shouted as they approached.

It has also been argued that it could have originated from basic European propaganda to ridicule and denigrate the movement. According to Kaggia (Kaggia, B, Leeuw and Kaggia M.) although Mau Mau had become the name by which the movement was known, they had no particular name for it in its early days. The name Muhimu meaning 'important' was coined by the Central Committee in order to disguise itself within KAU as people would often think that it meant KAU activities. The name was only known to members and it never went into newspapers. Mau Mau was always used by the European press.

This version is also supported by Barnett (1973) when he asserts:

> The very name 'Mau Mau' is an illustration of how successful propaganda can down an entire movement to which thousands sacrificed everything, including their lives, by attaching it to an appellation that conjures up all the clichés about the 'dark continent' which all concurs the European mind."

The ridicule and mockery of the movement is confirmed in the following sentence in the correspondence dated 14th September 1953 between the Provincial Information Officer, Central Province, and the executive officer of African information services: "I would advise you that the only thing I have produced outside your own campaign was 25 posters printed Keep Mau Mauth shut.

Though the movement was already being referred to as Mau Mau by the time of the active stage of resistance revolt against the British, it was only on 21st September 1948, according to a government official Cornfield (1960), that the name Mau Mau was mentioned in an official government document. The Kenyan historian and foremost Mau Mau scholar, Maina Wa Kinyatti (2008), also gives his account on the origin of the name Mau Mau:

> On May 12, 1950, thirty-nine Kenyan farm workers were arrested in Naivasha after nyapara Njihia wa Kinuthia reported to his white colonial employer S.V. Aitchison, that he had

been coerced by the arrested workers to join a secret organization whose political goal was to drive wazungu out of Kenya by violent means. Specifically, he informed Aitchison that the organization was using a traditional oath as a tool of recruitment, unity and commitment.

The 39 workers refused to reveal the aims and the name of the secret organization and were taken to court. During the court session one of the arrested workers, Magrougi ole Kodogoya, under crossexamination, absolutely refused to cooperate prosecutor and reveal the nature of the movement. The Magistrate angrily insisted that Kodogoya answer the question put to him by the prosecutor. Kodogoya firmly told the kangaroo magistrate 'Ndingikwira Maundu "Mau Mau "nderirwo ndikoige ni Kiama; ni hitho iitu.Ningi we uri thu iitu. Ni inyui mwatutunyire bururi na hinya,Mugitutua Ngombo cianyu. Bururi uyu ni witu twatigiirwo ni Aagu na Aagu.Tukikaurekia [I cannot reveal to you the aims and objectives of the movement. It is our secret. Besides, you are our enemy. You white people took our country by force and made us your slaves. This is our country; we inherited it from our ancestors. We shall never abandon.]

The prosecutor was not satisfied with Kodogoya's answer. He asked him, "Are you telling this court that the name of your secret society is 'Mau Mau'? I want an answer yes or no. "Instead of explaining to Kodogoya what the Prosecutor was asking, the interpreter told him, "Buana ndakwenda Uhoro Muingi; akwenda ucokie, I kana Aaca." (The boss does not want a detailed explanation to this question; he wants you to answer yes or no). Confused by the question, Kodogoya said, ''yes". This was a linguistic confusion, but out of this confusion and seeking a way to characterize the clandestine organization, the colonial English press seized upon the words Mau Mau as the name of the movement.

According to Maina Wa Kinyatti, the British Colonizers coined the term Mau Mau to insult, denigrate and debase the Kenyan anti-imperialist resistance. The freedom fighters, according to Kinyatti, only referred to themselves as the Kenya Land and Freedom Army (KLFA).

The different theories on the origin and meaning of the words Mau Mau infer that the words possibly did not have a particular meaning. The militant tag of Kenya land and freedom army is more accepted as the name for the Mau Mau freedom fighters.

References

Alao A., 2006, Mau Mau Warrior. Osprey Publishing. Peterborough Corfield, F.D., 1960, Historical Survey and the Origins and Growth of Mau Mau, H.M.Stationery Office,

Kaggia B, Leeuw W. Dee & Kaggia M, 2012, The struggle for freedom and Justice: The life and times of Bildad M. Kaggia, 1921- 2005, Nairobi, Trans Africa Press.

Kinyatti M, 2008, History of Resistance in Kenya 1884-2002, Mau Mau Research Center, Nairobi Kariuki .M., 1975, Mau Mau Detainee, Nairobi, Oxford University Press.

Muchai K., 1973, The story of Karigo Muchai, LSM Information Center, Richmond, Canada

Bildad Kaggia on Socialism

1. The main objective of socialism is to enable man to know the unjust economic conditions so as to stop the exploitation of one human being by another. An exploiter is an exploiter, whether an Asian, a Jew, an African or a Japanese. Any economic system whether you call it African Socialism or Arab Socialism which does not have the aim of ending the exploitation of man by man is not socialism.
2. All socialists are aiming at one ideal society — a classless society, just fellowship, cooperative and so on.
3. The most important thing is the means to achieve these objectives, which are essential to every socialist state. It is essential to end exploitation of man by man through public ownership of the means for production, distribution and exchange except during the transition period. If we leave the Kenya highlands to be owned individually we shall still have exploitation of man by man whether you say the Africans now own land there - so long as one man waits for the fruits of his employees and pays them a token wage - that is still capitalism whether black or white. What is important is that the means of production should be in the hands of the public and all people should share the natural wealth of their country and not leave it in the hand of a few rich foreigners, mainly Asians and Europeans.
4. What is essential to create a socialist state Kenya is to give equal opportunities to all citizens of the country to develop their intellectual talents to improve their health, to use their ability to earn a living.
5. One of the special circumstances is that the masses of Kenyan people have political power which is a vital weapon against any other exploiter. The difficult thing is whether people to whom the masses have given political power are socialist or capitalist at heart. Whatever it is, our party must be democratized. Our party officials must study socialism thoroughly and master the techniques of socialist economic planning and thereby be fully capable of piloting our socialist ship.

- Kaggia, Bildad M, W. de Leeuw and M. Kaggia (2012): The Struggle for Freedom and Justice: The Life and Times of the Freedom Fighter and Politician Bildad M. Kaggia (1921-2005). Nairobi: Transafrica Press.

Just Released

Durrani S., Waweru K. (2019) Kenya: Repression and Resistance from colony to Neo-colony 1948-1990. In: Ness I., Cope Z. (eds) The Palgrave Encyclopedia of Imperialism and Anti-Imperialism. Palgrave Macmillan, Cham. Available at: https://link.springer.com/referenceworkentry/10.1007/978-3-319-91206-6_9-1#howtocite.

Kenya Resists: Artists Challenge the Hawk in the Sky

Shiraz Durrani

The year is 1976. The nation is in the iron grip of a powerful KANU (Kenya African National Union) elite which tolerates no opposition to its tyrannical rule, nor any resistance to its anti-people policies. Anyone who dares to challenge the all-powerful armed might of the minority elite in power is detained, jailed, exiled, eliminated or disappeared. Those eliminated in early years of Uhuru for opposing land grabs and stealing of national wealth had included General Baimunge and Pio Gama Pinto (both 1965, see 'Biographies', below). JM Kariuki suffered the same fate in 1975. An overview of that year is provided by Carol Sicherman,[1] indicating the political situation in the country:

> 1975 (March): Disturbances follow assassination on 2 March of JM Kariuki; during student clashes with police, students are raped, nearly 100 students arrested, and dozens hospitalised …. 28 May: University of Nairobi closes following student disturbances …. 15 October: Martin Shikuku and Jean Marie Seroney, opposition MPs, are detained, gun being drawn on Seroney. On 16 October [President] Kenyatta warns his critics: 'People seem to forget that a hawk is always in the sky ready to swoop on the chicken.

In such an oppressive situation in 1976, the mass media dared not question the dictates of the regime. The looting of peasant land by 'legal means' was the order of the day. Key sectors of the economy were farmed out among the ruling elite, backed by murder gangs and the GSU[2] paramilitary force. Starvation, landlessness, unemployment and homelessness were the reality for working people. The key demands of Mau Mau – return of land, free education, medical care, freedom and political power – became distant dreams.

All avenues of protest were blocked. No party but KANU could be registered. Peasants could not complain about their stolen lands and unfair returns; workers had no militant trade unions – like the East African Trade Union Congress under Makhan Singh or the militants in the 1950s who introduced working class ideology to Mau Mau – which could represent their economic and political rights; professionals, civil servants, students, indeed nobody, had constitutional rights to life and liberty anymore. Life itself became a gift from the ruling class, not a right.

History books were closed, historians silenced. The regime felt threatened by the calls for socialism, justice and equality, fearing it could destroy the status quo. The aims of Mau Mau would destabilise the neo-colonial 'peace' for the elite. Armed resistance to colonialism and capitalism could not be mentioned. For what would happen if the same methods were used today? 'Forgive, and forget history' became the daily mantra from the ruling elite. We all fought for Uhuru, it claimed, even when homeguards who fought against the people and for the colonial masters were rewarded with state power. It was the time of torture, massacres and violent death. 'Follow what you are told or face the GSU' was the elite's message to the restless youth seeking justice. The country was turned into a prison without walls for the working class.

But wait. All is not silence. Resistance is taking root again as it must under all repression. Underground resistance is awakening once more. A forthcoming article[3] by Kimani Waweru and myself looks at the growth of this resistance:

> Most of the open spaces to express discontent were shut down …. In 1975 resistance regrouped and formed an underground party, the Kenya Workers' Party[4]. The party took a leftist stand and operated in utmost secrecy. Knowing too well that the people who were to bring genuine change were workers and peasants, it endeavoured to reach them and to learn from their experiences. They were the resistance, the real workers' party. It connected with working people through cultural activities. The most famous of their activities was theatre, and an example of this was Ngugi wa Thiong'o's play Ngaahika Ndeenda (I will marry when I want), which was performed in Limuru by peasants and workers. The play depicted the struggles of peasants and workers.

Recognising its power, the government of the day banned it and detained the writer. The detention of opponents of the ruling regime was the order of the day during the seventies. Among those who were detained were Koigi wa Wamwere, a young MP at the time, deputy speaker of the

National Assembly Jean Marie Seroney, another vocal MP, Martin Shikuku and George Anyona, among others.

The December Twelve Movement (DTM), successor to the Kenya Workers' Party, set out its ideological position. It became active in the three areas that were essential in any resistance movement: political, economic and cultural activities. It established study cells and linked its theories with practice. It was active in trade unions and started working with workers and peasants in their struggles. It radicalised professional bodies. It realised the importance of information and communications and published an underground newspaper, Pambana[5]. It also established a library underground, many of which books are in the Ukombozi Library today (see box). It was actively researching and publishing historical material. It was also active on many of the sorts of cultural front recently outlined by Len WMcCluskey[6] in the British context:

> There is another struggle, though – the cultural struggle. And culture is not just the arts, it is all the things we do to entertain, educate and enlighten ourselves, usually with others. It includes the arts like music, films, theatre and poetry.

As was the practice with all of DTM's work, its cultural policy and practice was influenced by theories from other revolutionary situations in Africa and elsewhere, such as the Soviet Union, China, Cuba and Vietnam. Particularly important was the use in its study sessions of Mao's Talks at the Yenan Forum on Literature.[7] At the same time, it circulated underground the history of Kenya from working class perspective and its vision of the society it was aiming for. This was later published as InDependent Kenya.[8]

DTM cells organised different types of activities, in different languages at different times. For example, they produced a children's play, Amaro Desh, Kenya (Our Country, Kenya) in Gujarati with child actors and actresses. Plays it produced included Portraits of Survival and Kinjikitile – Maji Maji [see Box 1]. Another activity was the showing of progressive films to workers and peasants, as I have recorded:[9]

> Among its early ventures was the showing of progressive films to workers and peasants in a semi-rural area just outside the city. The shows were organised by Sehemu [see Box 2] as part

of the work of the Kabete Library serving the Faculties of Agriculture and Veterinary Science of the University of Nairobi at the Kabete Campus, about 16 km from the city centre. The film shows were held in the lecture theatre at the campus and took place in 1981. This was an important departure for the progressive librarianship movement from the conservative service in Kenya in a number of ways. The use of film shows as a way of meeting information and learning needs of local communities was one such departure. Another was the fact that the doors of a major academic institution were opened for the first time to a non-academic – worker and peasant audience. But perhaps the most significant point was the content of the films. Three films were shown in the Black Man's Land trilogy: White Man's Country, Mau Mau and Kenyatta. These were produced and directed by Anthony Howarth and David R Koff and were written by David R Koff. The significance of showing these films was that they were frowned upon by the KANU Government at the time and even the normal showing of the films was extremely difficult, if not impossible.

DTM also encouraged its members to write plays, short stories and poems. Some poems were carried in Pambana. A collection of resistance poems was circulating underground and is to be published by Vita Books in 2019 under the title Tunakataa! (We Say No!). Kenyan history has failed to record not only the achievements of Mau Mau but also resistance to neocolonialism, capitalism and imperialism after independence. This includes the work of DTM in different fields. It is not surprising that the KANU-Moi government sought to eliminate DTM as it saw the real danger posed to the comprador rule, particularly as DTM mobilised thousands at its cultural activities.

Kenyan History Through Carvings
It was in this climate that a group of Wakamba wood carver artists, with the support of DTM activists, began to study Kenyan history. This was not easy, as few books on Mau Mau and the struggle against colonialism and imperialism were available. DTM's underground library filled the gap. The carvers' deep research revealed Mau Mau's real history and contribution to the war of independence. They then told Kenya's history by carving key scenes onto wood carvings. There were 36 carvings in all. The artists created multiple copies of the complete set which soon became collectors' items among DTM members and supporters. The entire collection was

1. Underground Libraries

The liberation forces of necessity had to set up their own underground liberation libraries. Perhaps the largest one was that run by Nazmi Durrani, which provided a major reference point for the December Twelve Movement. The library, in a safe house in Nairobi, contained material which was banned in Kenya andwhich could lead to indefinite detention if the owner was found out. This included works of Marx, Lenin, Stalin and Castro, as well as publications from the USSR and the Foreign Languages.

The library also provided the source material for important documents in the fight against the neocolonial Moi regime, such as *Mwakenya's Kenya, Register of Resistance (1987)*, and *Umoja-Kenya's 1989 publication, Moi's Reign of Terror*: a decade of Nyayo crimes against the people of Kenya [Nyayo House is a government skyscraper in Nairobi, notorious for its detention chambers in the basement.] The safe house also became a centre of cyclostyling and distribution for the second issue of Pambana, published in July 1983. Cell members used motorbikes, cars, bicycles and public transport to distribute the newspapers to other cadres as well as to members of the public. The Ukombozi Library was established in Nairobi by the Kenya chapter of the Progressive African Library and Information Activists' Group (PALIAct) in partnership with Vita Books and the Mau Mau Research Centre. PALIAct's publicity states:

> PALIAct is an initiative of a group of progressive African librarians and information workers. We recognise that current leaders in the African information field have done little to break the colonial and imperialist policies and practices in meeting the information needs of working people in Africa, or to make the profession more relevant to the needs of African librarians and information workers."
> The Library incorporates the December Twelve Movement's underground library. It aims to make available progressive material and to encourage reading, study and research by working people in Kenya. The need for such a library follows from the fact that progressive literature has been generally ignored by most libraries and learning institutions. Young people with a passion to bring about improvement in the country and a thirst for materials that would inspire them in their quest for social justice get disappointed as such materials are hard to come by. The Ukombozi Library has an initial collection of almost a thousand titles of progressive material, mostly books but also pamphlets, videos and photographs. A majority of these are classics which are either out of print or cannot be found in the local bookshops. Other material has been donated by the Mau Mau Research Centre, Vita Books and many progressive individuals active in the information struggle in Kenya.

2. Sehemu ya Utungaji

"The Creative Wing" was a group of patriotic Kenyan librarians in the 1980s associated with the University of Nairobi Library Magazine. They felt that the information services then were a continuation of colonial practices and had not been changed to answer the needs of the people of Kenya. The Sehemu brought together all creative activities, ranging from painting, drawing, creative writing, creative awareness through film shows, plays etc, generating new ideas which they aimed to translate into action.

The Sehemu group was planning to produce books on Mau Mau leaders but came to an early end in 1984. Before that, however, it had formed a partnership with a Nairobi drama group, Takhto Arts, to produce the play Kinjikitile, Maji Maji. This dealt with the Tanzanian people's war of liberation against German colonialism, 1904-1907, conducted by the Maji Maji movement and led by Kinjikitile. "Maji" is the Kiswahili term for water and was used at the time as a call for unity. The script of the play was taken from Kinjikitile, by Tanzanian author Ebrahim Hussein (1969), but adapted by Naila Durrani and Shiraz Durrani to reflect Kenyan reality.

on exhibition for a month at the YMCA (Young Men's Christian Association) Cottage Crafts, Nairobi in 1976 and attracted thousands of students and workers.

As the exhibition did not attract mainstream politicians' attention, it was not banned. However, many of the carvings are currently lost as activists who had collected them faced increasing repression and had to distribute them among supporters. They are likely to be in the homes of workers and peasants today, but as far as is known, no library, archive ormuseum in Kenya has the collection – another reflection of the neo-colonial control over people's culture. Settler and foreign artwork is easy to find in Kenya today, but sadly the same does not apply to Kenya's artwork. The accompanying images reproduce some of the ones rescued from imperialist claws.

What thus emerged on the art and historical fronts was truly remarkable. At one level, the carvings demolished the ruling classes' embargo on protest and resistance – here was the real history of Kenya which had been silenced since independence. At another level, they used a form where no words were written, no embargoes broken – yet history was there for all to see. It mattered not whether one had reading skills or not, whether one was fluent in English or not. The form and content were in perfect harmony, to give visual evidence of the heroic struggle. The neocolonial embargo on history, on information, on communications was totally broken. While historians could not do research or disseminate the results of their research to the people whose history they were working on, this group of artist-scholars created the history of the hidden aspects of Mau Mau. They highlighted the key vision of the movement which challenged the colonial and imperialist-induced social values. They explained their position on burning issues of the day and threw light on the historical approaches to resolving social contradictions.

Resistance Art

The neocolonial setup in Kenya in 1976 had ensured that people's art and culture served only tourist markets, divorcing them from lives of working classes. The wood art of the Kamba nationality had been one of the victims of the attacks on people's customs and cultures. It was gradually depoliticised by market forces, which became the new rulers under capitalism and imperialism. Tourists do not want politics, just items of what they consider 'beauty', and the Wakamba artists began producing wood carving of animals which satisfied the tourist and overseas markets. The needs of the Kenyan people remained ignored. Until, that is, the youthful group of the activist carvers broke the embargo imposed by the market economy. They pioneered a new art form with relevant content in their revolutionary wood carvings. They put politics in command once more in art.

For all their achievements, the artists remain almost unknown in Kenyan history today. They were Mule wa Musembi, Kitonyi wa Kyongo, Kitaka wa Mutua and Mutunga wa Musembi. The exhibition was curated by Sultan Somjee from the University of Nairobi.

Little was known in Kenya about the history of Mau Mau in 1976 as research and publication on it had been suppressed by the government. It is therefore interesting to see the carvings dig out key aspects of Mau Mau. These include their ideology, their strategies and tactics, their actions, development of technologies, record keeping and communications, leadership as well as their attitude to women, nationalities and their class perspective. The write-up accompanying the exhibition contained historical facts not commonly known except to Mau Mau activists. For example, a team of two or more Mau Mau activists would carry messages from the Mau Mau High Command in the heart of Nyandarua to different Mau Mau centres, and to its armies, or to the progressive workers and peasants throughout the country. The carving project brought such facts to the public. The text accompanying Carving No 1 (unfortunately not included here) records the tactics of Mau Mau in communication when confronted by enemy soldiers:[10]

Two couriers carrying orders from the Kenya Defence Council are caught in the enemy ambush. One courier rushes at the enemy so that the other may escape and deliver the orders. The dying fighter digs deep the soil and exhorts his companion to continue. The courier crosses many ridges and valleys across Kenya.

With works like these, Kenyan artists became trendsetters in resistance art.

This article is a much extended version of the author's 'Mau Mau Wood Carvings Narrative', which appeared in Awaaz magazine Kenya, Vol 15, issue 3, 2018, pp 1-4. Fig 1 is reproduced with kind permission from Awaaz; Figs 1, 2, 4 and 5 are © Shiraz Durrani.

Biographies of cited Kenyan political activists

GENERAL BAIMUNGE (19??-1965) was a Mau Mau general, and deputy to Dedan Kimathi. He refused to leave the forest at independence in 1963, demanding that the government give free land, jobs and assistance to Mau Mau. He was killed on 26 January 1965 "at the hands of the Uhuru (independent) government" of Jomo Kenyatta.[11]

PIO GAMA PINTO (1927-1965) was a trade unionist, journalist and nationalist. He was an anticolonial activist in Goa (then under Portuguese rule) and Kenya and was active in the Mau Mau liberation movement. After independence in Kenya, he continued his anti-imperialist struggle and supported socialism. He was assassinated on 24 February 1965.[12]

JOSIAH MWANGI KARIUKI (1929-1975) was a Mau Mau detainee, later a Member of Parliament. "In later years he became a widely popular spokesman for the peasantry and the poor, claiming that 'we do not want a Kenya of ten millionaires and ten million beggars' … he was brutally murdered on 2 March 1975. When he was killed he was campaigning against corruption and actively opposing the political leadership … 'there was no doubt whatever that high authorities in Kenya were responsible for his murder'"

MARTIN SHIKUKU (1963-2012) was a Kenyan Member of Parliament from 1963 to1988. "Seen as a radical, he early declared himself 'President of the Poor'. He paid for his prolonged opposition with detention in October 1975. He was adopted by Amnesty International as a prisoner of conscience. He was released in December 1978."[14] "In KANU, Shikuku gained a reputation as an outspoken backbencher, critical of corruption and abuses of power, and a defender of parliamentary privileges."[15]

JEAN MARIE SERONEY (1925-1982) was Deputy Speaker of the Kenyan Parliament in 1975, when his support of Shikuku's declaration that "KANU has been killed" led to his detention; he was adopted by Amnesty International as a prisoner of conscience. He was released in December 1978.[16]

MAKHAN SINGH JABBAL (1913-1973) has previously been profiled in this journal.[17] He was, according to Carol Sicherman, a "Pre-eminent trade union leader. Secretary of the Labour Trade Union of Kenya when he organised a two-month strike in Nairobi (1937). Interned in India for five years (1940-1945). In 1949, he founded the East African Trade Union Congress with Fred Kubai. He was arrested in 1950 and restricted until 1961. His attempt to enter the trade union movement [after his release] was banned by the new leaders (after independence) 'suspicious of his socialist' leanings. He spent his final years writing a two-volume history of the [trade union] movement."[18] While in India, 1939-47, he was a member of the Communist Party and edited its newspaper. His son Hindpal says:

"My father, Makhan Singh … shall always be remembered as the father of the labour movement in Kenya. And since the labour movement was closely interwoven with the political movement in the colonial period, my father was also a great nationalist. He was amongst the first ones to use the slogan 'Uhuru sasa', meaning 'Freedom Now', in his famous speech in April 1950, at Kaloleni Hall, just a few days before his arrest and long detention by the Colonial Government in remote parts of Kenya, for more than eleven years."[19]

NGUGI WA THIONG'O is an award-winning, world-renowned Kenyan writer and academic who writes primarily in Gikuyu. His work includes novels, plays, short stories, and essays, ranging from literary and social criticism to children's literature. He is the founder and editor of the Gikuyu-language journal Mutuiri. In 1977, Ngugi embarked upon a novel form of theatre in his native Kenya that sought to liberate the theatrical process from what he held to be "the general bourgeois education system", by encouraging spontaneity and audience participation in the performances. His project sought to "demystify" the theatrical process, and to avoid the "process of alienation [that] produces a gallery of active stars and an undifferentiated mass of grateful admirers" which, according to Ngugi, encourages passivity in "ordinary people". Although his landmark play, Ngaahika Ndeenda, co-written with Ngugi wa Mirii, was a commercial success, it was shut down by the authoritarian Kenyan regime six weeks after its opening. Ngugi wa Thiong'o was subsequently imprisoned for over a year. Adopted as an Amnesty International prisoner of conscience, he was released from prison, and fled Kenya.[20] For further information see Carol Sicherman's book. [21]

KOIGI WA WAMWERE (1949-) is a Kenyan politician, human rights activist, journalist and writer. He became famous for opposing both the Jomo Kenyatta and Daniel arap Moi regimes, both of which sent him to detention.[22]

GEORGE ANYONA (1945-2003) was elected an MP in 1977, but later that year was detained without trial by then President Jomo Kenyatta. Although released in 1978 by President Daniel arap Moi, he was arrested again in 1982, along with his longtime friend and veteran politician Jaramogi Oginga Odinga The two were detained without trial for attempting to form a political party, the Kenya African Socialist Alliance (KASA), to challenge the ruling party KANU. Shortly after their arrest, KANU pushed through a constitutional amendment, making Kenya a de facto one-party state. Released from detention in 1984, Anyona made a political comeback in 1990 during the clamour for multi-party democracy in Kenya. However, he was then arrested with several others on a charge of sedition.

After a marathon trial, the defendants were jailed for seven years. It was later revealed by an assistant minister in the Office of the President, John Keen, that the allegations were nothing but government fabrications, and in 1992 the defendants were released on bail and then had theirsentences quashed.[23]

Women in Struggle: Armed Mau Mau women fighters marching into action.

Manufacture: Mau Mau inventors and technicians in a gun factory in a cave

Women's role is in the struggle: Protect family, collect food and confront homeguards

Democracy: Decisions made in meetings while ready to confront enemy: Kenya Defence Council meeting.

War of independence: British fighter jets are powerless to stop resistance

Mau Mau activists continue their resistance while homeguards look for them in vain.

Colonial justice: Fearless fighter confronts judge and armed homeguard: The trial of Dedan Kimathi

Multi-nationality Mau Mau forces: Senior Chief Mukudi of Samia and Bunyala with Mau Mau fighters

Notes and References

1. C Sicherman, Ngugi wa Thiong'o: the making of a rebel: a source book in Kenyan literature and resistance, Hans Zell, Documentary Research in African Literature, London, 1990, pp 90-91.

2. GSU = General Services Unit. "Prime Minister Jomo Kenyatta started to build up GSU as a counter-balance to the army. President Moi also became more dependent on the GSU, which eventually gained the reputation of being the military arm of the executive branch, an allegation that continues to this day. Some of the GSU's more controversial activities occurred in the months prior to the 1992 and 1997 general elections when its personnel mobilised against pro-democracy advocates and other anti-government elements." – Maxon and Ofcansky, qv, pp 82-83.

3. S. Durrani and K Waweru, Kenya: Repression and Resistance: From Colony to Neo-Colony, 1948-1990 (forthcoming).

4. The Kenya Workers' Party later became the December Twelve Movement, later still, Mwakenya (Union of Patriots for the Liberation of Kenya, known in Swahili as Muunganowa Wazalendowa Kukomboa Kenya).

5. Pambana is Kiswahili for "struggle".

6. L McCluskey, Foreword to On Fighting On: An anthology of poems from the Bread and Roses Poetry Award, Culture Matters, London, 2017.

7. Mao Tse-tung, Talks at the Yenan Forum on Literature and Art (1942), in Selected Works, Vol IV, Lawrence & Wishart, 1956; online at https://www.marxists.org/reference/archive/mao/selected-works/volume-3/mswv3_08.htm.

8. InDependent Kenya was circulated in cyclostyled form in Kenya in 1981. In 1982 it was published in London by Zed Press and sponsored by the Journal of African Marxists "in solidarity with the authors".

9. S. Durrani, Progressive Librarianship: Perspectives from Kenya and Britain, 1979-2010, Vita Books, Nairobi, p 131. 7

10 Publicity leaflet, History of Kenya, 1952-1958: A guide to the exhibition by Kenyan artists Mule wa Musembi, Kitonyi wa Kyongo, Kitaka wa Mutua and Mutunga wa Musembi, held at Cottage Crafts, Nairobi in 1976.

11 Sicherman, op cit, p 105, quoting sources.

12 See S Durrani, Pia Gama Pinto: Kenya's Unsung Martyr 1927-1965, Vita Books, Kenya, 2018, reviewed by C Fernandes in CR90, Winter 2018-2019, pp 23-26.

13. Sicherman, op cit, pp 125-6, quoting sources.

14. Ibid, p 178.

15. RM Maxon and TP Ofcansky, Historical Dictionary of Kenya (African Historical Dictionaries, No 77), Scarecrow, Langham, MD, 2d edn, 2000, p 235.

16. Sicherman, op cit, p 177.

17. See S Durrani, 'Reflections on the Revolutionary Legacy of Makhan Singh in Kenya', Autumn 2014, pp 10-17.

18. Sicherman, op cit, pp 178-9.

19 S Durrani, Makhan Singh: A Revolutionary Kenyan Trade Unionist, Vita Books, Nairobi, 2015, p 15.

20.See https://en.wikipedia.org/wiki/Ngũgĩ wa Thiong%27o.

21. Sicherman, op cit.

22. See https://en.wikipedia.org/wiki/Koigi_wa_Wamwere.

23. See https://en.wikipedia.org/wiki/George_Anyona.

Freedom & Democracy

…Freedom and democracy do not exist in the abstract, only in the concrete. In a society rent by class struggle, if there is freedom for the exploiting classes to exploit the working people, there is no freedom for the working people not to be exploited, and if there is democracy for the bourgeoisie, there is no democracy for the proletariat and other working people... Those who demand freedom and democracy in the abstract regard democracy as an end and not a means. Democracy sometimes seems to be an end, but it is in fact only a means. - Mao Zedong

We must secure for the workers and peasant farmers the full fruits of their industry and the most equitable distribution thereof by ensuring that the means of production, distribution and exchange are under the best obtainable system and administration. Because K.A.N.U. is dedicated to the establishment of the above conditions it shall strive to promote a social and political order based on social, economic and political justice. — Kenya African National Union (1960): The K.A.N.U. Manifesto, 1960.

Our achievement of Independence, for which we have struggled for so long, will not be an end in itself. It will give us the opportunity to work unfettered for the creation of a democratic African socialist Kenya … Socialist because political freedom and equality are not enough. Our people have the right to be free from economic exploitation and social inequality. We aim to build a country where men and women are motivated by a sense of service and not driven by a greedy desire for personal gains. Everyone of you has a duty to help to create this nation. You must strive to exercise your rights fully and with understanding - Kenya African National Union (1960): The K.A.N.U. Manifesto.

Ideology - Ideas that can Oppress or Liberate

by Kimani Waweru

The word 'ideology', originated in France and according to John Plamenatz, It meant the science or study of ideas, and was first used to refer to a type of philosophy fashionable at the turn of the eighteenth and nineteenth centuries.[1] As the word started to be used internationally it changed and today it does not have a single clear definition but largely it is defined as set of opinions or political beliefs of a society or an individual. The human society has different classes and each class has its own ideas about the world (ideology). The ideology of the ruling class is usually the dominant one in a society. This is because the class has economic, political and legal power under its wing. The ideology of a ruling class reflects the material interest of the class which is to keep the status quo intact. It thus contributes to shaping the ideology of a society. Although the ideology of the ruling class is dominant, it is normally challenged by ideology of the working class. The challenge manifests as class struggle. The history of human beings is one of class struggles.

In modern times, there have been attempts to group ideological differences within the society into two social trends, i.e. left and right. The right wing is an ideology that is mostly associated with the conservatives i.e. those who block change in order to cling on to their privileges and power. The right wing or the conservatives - believes there is no way that society can be changed from the way it is currently. The left wing ideology is associated with working class. They do want to change the status quo and put in place a society where the principle of social justice and equality prevails. The history of human society has shown that people with these ideas have to a large extent been suppressed by the dominant class. Ultimately though, their ideas win as they conform to the reality. During feudalism in Europe, for example, landlords and the church were against the ideology of capitalists which was advocating change. The capitalists' ideology, being progressive at that time, won. However, the capitalist ideologists today, just as the feudal ideologists they overthrew, believe that there is no way that capitalist society can change. This therefore means they have ceased to be revolutionaries and have become reactionaries. It is on this basis that it will be important to understand the ideology of the working class which advocates change.

The Ideology of Working Class

The working class, being the victims of the status quo will ultimately yearn for change. This is the reason they are attracted to the ideology that advocates change. This, however, does not mean that the entire working class supports the ideology as there are other factors in society that hinder them, such as the ruling class propaganda, deception etc. The working class ideology is guided by the philosophy or principles of dialectical materialism. Dialectical materialism considers the world not as static or unchanging but as a continuous process of development in which things come into being and pass away. It strives to show that the driving force of this development is internal and not external. For example, the defeat of feudals by the capitalists was not due to military prowess of capitalists, though it (military) played a role, but rather due to the development of productive forces that broke limits set by the feudal system i.e. undermining the natural economy under feudal society. Dialectical materialism guides us in understanding that the defeat of capitalism is imminent. This is due to the internal contradiction within capitalism where the socially produced wealth is in contradiction with private appropriation of that wealth. The capitalists ignorantly claim that the contradiction between them and the workers is caused by external and not internal factors and accuse revolutionaries of inciting workers against them, thus forgetting that workers are forced to resist due to the internal contradiction of capitalism that constitutes the main basis. The role of revolutionaries is secondary and it comes into play because there is the basis which is inequality in distribution of social wealth. As Mao argued in his article on contradiction

materialist dialectics holds that external causes are the condition of change and internal causes are the basis of change, and that external causes become operative through internal causes. In a suitable temperature an egg changes into a chicken, but no temperature can change a stone into a chicken, because each has a different basis[2].

Materialism dialectics, as Mao said, shows us that changes in society are caused by the development of the internal contradictions in society. i.e. the contradiction between the productive forces and the relations of production. This contradiction pushes society forward and gives the impetus for the suppression of the old society by the new.

In short, dialectical materialism can be said to be a true scientific world outlook that is based on considering things as they are (in motion) without preconceived or idealistic assumptions. As Maurice Cornforth said, dialectical materialism insists that conceptions of things must be based on actual investigation and experience and must be constantly tested and retested in the light of practice and further practice. The principles of science have proved that the world can be explained and understood in terms of material causes without bringing in superstitions and myths.

Science and Socialism

Socialism should not be based on utopia i.e. dreaming of an ideal society without showing how it can be achieved[3]. Many progressives have fallen into this trap of trying to fit an idea which they assume is perfect into a system. For example, President Nyerere came up with the idea of Ujamaa (African socialism) in the late sixties. In his opinion, this was socialism based on the African traditions of communalism. The idea, though bringing some positive aspects in the country, failed to work due to it being unscientific. Socialism should be scientific. As Maurice Cornforth said, it should be based on an analysis of the actual movement of history, economic law of motion of capitalist society, thus showing how it arises as the necessary next stage in the evolution of a society, and how it can come about only by waging of the working class struggle, through the defeat of the capitalist class and the institution of the dictatorship of the working class[4] (socialism). Ideological understanding and analysis helps us to understand that the capitalist system has reached its limit and this can be authenticated by the unending economic crises. The capitalists and the ruling class are therefore forced to come up with deceptive defense mechanisms geared to whitewashing the face of capitalism. Some of these mechanisms include social welfare programmes (e.g. free or subsidized medical and education services).This is well executed in Europe especially among the Scandinavian countries. These programmes, however, keep being eroded day after day by capitalism, especially today when capitalism is not facing any serious threat as during the Soviet Union and the Cold War era.

Why ideology is important in liberation

Ideology based on scientific understanding will help the working class discover the true nature of capitalism which is concealed under a deceptive veneer of welfare to humanity. The discovery will ultimately illuminate the path to a new, better era.

The capitalist system is pregnant and it only needs a trained midwife, not a quack, to bring to birth the new era. By this I mean it needs well-grounded cadres with scientific understanding of a society who are able to navigate through the complexities of capitalism with the goal of leading the masses to socialism.

Endnotes

1 Plamenatz J., 1970, Ideology – Key Concepts in Political Science, Pall Mall Press Ltd, London, , p. 15

2 Tse Tung M., 1971, On Contradiction – Selected Readings from the Work of Mao Tse Tung, Foreign Language Press, China , p. 89

3 Maurice Cornforth quote

4 Cornforth M., 1968, Materialism and the Dialectical Method, 4th edn., International Publishers Co., USA, p. 122

Socialism

As a body of ideas and as a movement toward a society beyond capitalism, Marxist socialism stands for the dissolution of capitalist private property, collective ownership of the means of production and distribution, a democratically planned economy and the replacement of antagonistic social relations of exploitation, competition and domination with relations of equality, co-operation and solidarity: a classless, communist society. From the Marxist perspective, socialism is not merely an ethical ideal: it is the only fully rational response to the intensifying contradictions of the capitalist world order. Socialism aims at eliminating the deeply entrenched material inequalities between classes, 'races,' nations and genders — that have been fostered and perpetuated by all class-antagonistic modes of production, inequalities that have reached truly monstrous proportions in the world capitalist system. Its goal is not the 'formal equality' sanctified by liberalism —a merely juridical and legal equality, which effaces and ignores the persistent differences that distinguish human beings in their concrete circumstances. Rather, its goal is to achieve a global society in which, in the words of The Communist Manifesto, 'the free development of each is the condition for the free development of all.' — Smith, Murray E. G and Joshua D. Dumont (2011): Socialist strategy yesterday and today: Notes on classical Marxism and the contemporary radical left. in: Veltmeyer, Henry, Ed. (2011): 21st Century Socialism: Reinventing the project. Pontypool: Merlin Press. pp. 119-138.

Ukombozi Library-A Speech During All African Peoples' Conference 2018

by Njoki Wamai

All African Peoples Conference was held in Accra Ghana from 5th to 8th December 2018. The conference was organised in collaboration with the the Trades Union Congress (TUC) of Ghana, the Socialist Forum of Ghana (SFG), Third World Network-Africa and Lincoln University, USA. It was to encourage participants to engage in open and dispassionate reflection on the African condition in the contemporary world, against the backdrop of the 1958 conference. More than 300 delegates drawn from different countries in Africa as well as members of the African descent from foreign states were also represented. Njoki Wamai a member of Ukombozi Library Committee represented the library. The following is the speech she delivered.

Africa's information has been captured and held by forces of imperialism. People do not have access to relevant information - all they are fed by imperialist-dominated mass media, public libraries and educational institutions is information from the point of view of capitalism and that which supports the ruling classes, African and foreign. Their constant message is TINA - There is No Alternative to capitalism and imperialism. This message is then reinforced by not allowing information about resistance to capitalism and imperialism taking place around the world from reaching the people in relevant form and language. Socialism is a non-existent subject in public domain under this system. The same goes for information, outlook, vision that drove Kenya's war of independence. Mau Mau is either not mentioned or made to look incompetent and without a clear ideology. Its leaders are demonised. The situation that imperialism is trying to silence is exactly what Mau Mau warned about:

> Kenya's Uhuru must not be transformed into freedom to exploit, or freedom to be hungry, and live in ignorance. Uhuru must be Uhuru for the masses — Uhuru from exploitation, from ignorance, disease and poverty (Pio Gama Pinto,1963).

This message is too dangerous for ruling classes so it is suppressed under the control systems on information.

Public Libraries are deprived of resources by comprador regimes which have money for vast projects from which they gain massive kickbacks but not for libraries. Progressive libraries which can widen perspectives and expand people's horizons are non-existent. The model of public libraries set up by colonialism has remained in a "free" Kenya. These do not meet the information needs of Africa's workers, peasants, and other working people.

The key point to emphasise is that under colonial and neo-colonial models that has been imposed on Africa/Kenya, there are sharp class divisions with the power handed over to a comprador clique and working people deprived not only of their land, livelihood, health care, education that their fight for independence was all about, but their information needs as well. Public libraries are forced to depend on material donated by overseas publishers and these do not challenge the status quo. The British Council, USIS and other agencies from France, Germany and other imperialist powers then have a field day filling minds of Kenyans with ideas and experiences that glorify capitalism and imperialism while suppressing liberation information from Kenya, Africa and around the world. African traditional information systems which satisfied people's information needs in an earlier period have not been allowed to adopt to new needs. They have either been suppressed or made to serve capitalist needs.

Resistance in Information and Communication

The above situation has generated a large amount of resistance by working people in Kenya. Workers, peasants, students and many other organised groups have sought their own ways of resisting the imprisonment of their minds and their country. Among them are progressive information workers, students, political activists and their organisation. They reasoned that institutions established by neo-colonialism and ruling classes cannot, and will not, liberate their minds. They saw the essence of Assata Shakur's guidance:

> No one is going to give you the education you need to overthrow them. Nobody is going to teach you your true history, teach you your true heroes, if they know that that knowledge will help set you free.

It is on this basis that the Ukombozi Library was set up in 2017 by the Progressive African Library and Information Activists' Group (PALIAct) in partnership with Vita Books and the Mau Mau Research Centre in Nairobi. The Library aims to make available progressive material and to encourage reading, study and research by working people in Kenya. The need for such a library follows from the fact that progressive literature has been generally ignored by most libraries and learning institutions.

The Ukombozi Library has an initial collection of almost a thousand titles of progressive material, mostly books but also pamphlets, videos and photographs. A majority of these are classics which are either out of print or cannot be found in the local bookshops. Other material has been donated by Mau Mau Research Centre, Vita Books and many progressive individuals active in the information struggle in Kenya.

The Ukombozi Library has initiated the Community ReachOut project which breaks the colonial library mould and takes the library to various communities to enhance personal and national development. Community groups, libraries and institutions are welcomed to be institutional members of the Ukombozi Library. The institutional members borrow up to 5 titles from the Ukombozi Library for a maximum of 2 months. This initiative has already started with Mathare Social Justice Centre.

Membership is open to all who agree with the vision and principles of the library, irrespective of class, ethnicity, religion, gender, region, race or disability. Individuals or institutional membership is available on payment of [or the] appropriate fee. A number of people have registered majority being social justice activists. Members borrows materials for a period of two weeks. The library has a management committee which enhances efficiency and effectiveness in it service to the members as well as working people. The library is located on the Second Floor of University Way House (Uni House) next to Lilian Towers Hotel (Safari Club) along University Way.

People who pronounce themselves in favor of the method of legistlative reform in place of and in contradiction to the conquest of political power and social revolution, do not really choose a more tranquil, calmer and slower road to the same goal, but a different goal. Instead of taking a stand for the established of a new society they take a stand for surface modifications of the old society.... Our program becomes not the realization of Socialism, but the reform of capitalism; not the suppression of the system of the wage labor, but the diminution of exploitation, that is, the suppression of the abuses of capitalism instead of the suppression of capitalism itself.— Rosa Luxemburg, Reform or Revolution

There is no democracy without socialism, and no socialism without democracy.

Bourgeois society stands at the crossroads, either transition to socialism or regression into barbarism.

Selected Books Available at the Ukombozi Library

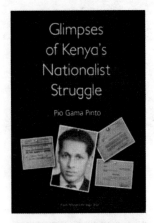

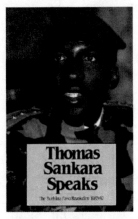

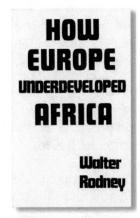

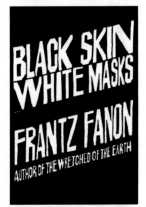

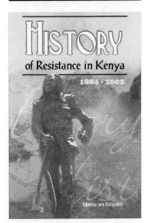

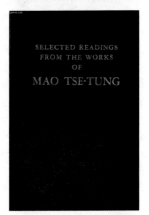

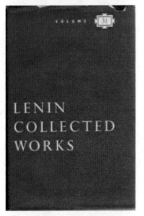

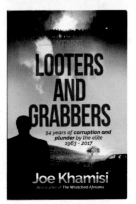

INTERVIEW: Shiraz Durrani interviewed on Information as a Tool of Liberation

Questions from Julian Jaravata. an MLIS student at San Jose State University taking a course in international librarianship. Interview date: 07-12-2018.

The interview took place in the context of Julian Jaravata's research for his librarianship studies. However the issues that arose related to the role of information in society and particularly the use of information as a tool of oppression by imperialism - and also as a tool of liberation in the hands of those resisting imperialism. It is this dual nature of information that can sometimes lead to misunderstanding its role in societies. Some additional points are reproduced at the end of the interview from lorraine churn's Reflections on Learning from the 2018 Creative Commons Summit as they make relevant points discussed in this interview.

Questions from Julian Jaravata.

1. In what ways you see progressive librarianship as a distinct field from international librarianship, but also the different ways in which they relate.

An important issue raised by your question is perhaps conceptual: progressive librarianship is seen in contrast to international librarianship. Is this appropriate? The real contradiction is between national and international progressive librarianship (socialist-orientated), and national and international conservative librarianship (capitalist-orientated). This opens up the possibility of both, the national AND international librarianship being progressive and socialist-orientated — whereas the current situation is that national and international librarianship are conservative and capitalist-orientated. This needs to be at the centre of any studies on international librarianship.

Let us understand the real meaning and purpose of "progressive librarianship" (PL). PL has arisen in response to the traditional librarianship (TL) model developed under capitalism and propagated internationally by imperialism. TL has been promoted as the only possible model of librarianship and so goes without the defining term "conservative" before the name, thus becoming the universal term "librarianship". In this context, even the term "conservative" is inadequate and should be replaced by capitalist librarianship as opposed to socialist librarianship.

In view of the embargo on the concept and ideals of socialism placed by capitalism and imperialism, it has been difficult for those seeking an alternative to CL to call the alternative Socialist Librarianship as that would make it difficult to put it into practice because of the power of finance capital. I recall that when I first started working in UK at Hackney Public Libraries in 1987, the term socialist library was used quite often, until the attacks on any alternative to capitalism under Maggie Thatcher's Conservative government made it difficult to use even the term, socialism. That began the TINA era - There is No Alternative to capitalism and full-scale attacks began on any progressive developments in libraries - or in any other field.

Now, if we accept that the PL movement in general aspires to socialist ideals of justice and equality for working classes and those oppressed by capitalism, then it follows that issues of classes, class conflicts and class struggles are central concerns for PL. Without this, it remains a meaningless jargon used to create a false sense of "alternatives" to CL. So it is important to understand that PL without class analysis is a meaningless term.

In that scenario, International Librarianship (IL) gains new significance. It is not a question of whether PL is "a distinct field from international librarianship". PL sees the struggle of working classes against capitalism and imperialism in its national as well as in its internationalist contexts. Capitalism is not confined to one country. Imperialism, by its very nature, is also not confined to one country. They have global approach and global reach. For PL to be effective in one country, it has, of necessity, to link up with PL movements in other countries and globally if it is to be an effective social force. This implies that PL has to link up and work in solidarity with the struggles of working classes in its own, as well as, in other countries.

The situation that PL faces is the oppression of working classes by capitalism and imperialism. It cannot resolve this by ignoring its real enemies. For this it needs to work with its class allies internally and internationally.

This understanding of PL and its social and international context may be problematic for some PL organisations in that they are in countries which officially follow capitalism and are against socialism. But PL work, of necessity, involves engaging in class struggles in their society. The issue is how to challenge capitalism/imperialism in the library and information world. Some may do it openly, others stealthily, but the fundamental contradiction that PL address are the same.

The progressive librarianship movements in USA and Europe, as well as in some countries of Africa has developed links with each other and a recent publication by Al Kagan[1] records their history and aims. Such activities have strengthened these organisations individually as well as the PL movement internationally.

The elephant in the room for international librarianship, as for national librarianship, is capitalism and imperialism. Once this is fully recognised, there will be clarity on where librarianship needs to go. Progressive librarianship can then be seen as a step towards non-capitalist or socialist library service from the present capitalist/conservative setup. That is the key struggle in librarianship today, for both, national and international librarianship. The power relations between capitalist/conservative librarianship and progressive/socialist librarianship can then be seen more clearly — both nationally and internationally.

2. Along those lines, what have been your experiences working with across different borders, both regionally within Africa as well as throughout the globe, with progressive librarian networks?

The situation of **Britain** is that of a country brought development and growth by plundering the resources of the entire world under the so-called British Empire. This was a glorified term for global looting, massacres and plunder. The loot enabled the rich and powerful to amass massive wealth and the crumbs from their table ensured that the revolutionary flames of working class were not allowed to engulf the entire country. But the situation began to change gradually with the decline of the Empire under resistance from the conquered countries. As countries achieved independence, the power of the empire to syphon off wealth of workers and peasants declined. This is when neo-colonialism replaced colonialism but for Britain the change was more traumatic as the new imperialist power, USA, muscled in for its share of the loot. This further weakened British capitalism and reduced its ability to suppress militancy among working classes.

The PL movement in Britain when I started working in 1987 reflected the state of the country - conservative. Than there was very conservative professional body, the British Library Association[2] which later changed its name to CILIP[3]. It was part of the national establishment and saw no need to challenge the status quo, politically or in the context of libraries and the needs of librarians. There were no specific trade unions for library workers who then joined national trade unions. While they protected the interests of librarians as workers, there was no organisation that took on the broader role of questioning the general direction of libraries, public or academic.

My experiences in UK and Kenya are recorded in my books, Progressive Librarianship[4] and Information and Liberation[5]. In general, it was a struggle where progressive librarianship won some battles and created liberated territories which flourished while there was political, trade union and community power behind the initiatives (as in the Three Continents Liberation Collection in Hackney[6]) or the progressive staffing structure and the the Innovations Project in Merton. But as power shifted nationally to the Conservative party, such initiatives were rendered powerless and were closed down or forced to die out for lack of support and funds.

Perhaps a better approach was in changing the teaching curricula at the London Metropolitan University where a progressive approach was adopted. This addressed the key issue of training progressive staff from the early stages of their professional career. Another initiative was the Quality Leaders Project -Youth which developed management skills of library staff while developing progressive services too. The Project proved successful in four or five libraries nationally, Yet even here, the policies of the Conservative Government ensured that such initiatives were also suppressed as they posed real challenges to the capitalist model.

All this indicated the need for librarians to be active in the political as well as professional fields if they are to be successful.

Kenya lost an opportunity to build a people-oriented library service at independence.[7] With the "aid" of the departing colonial power, it strengthened the conservative model of libraries, both public and academic. Several attempts to introduce progressive library and information activities are recorded in my two books mentioned earlier.

It was only in 2017 that a total departure took place when the Progressive African Library and Information Activists' Group (PALIAct) set up the Ukombozi Library in Nairobi. The Ukombozi Library has a sizeable collection of progressive books and is establishing strong links through it ReachOut Project to link up with local working class communities and students.

Here again, there is no official government support and the public library service continues it "traditional" approach, unconnected with any progressive movement.

3. Given the particular way that PALIAct asserts itself as an activist organization that emphasizes serving workers and peasants, what are lessons from your experiences that might be able to be offered to other countries with class relations that may bear some similarities? (For me, the discussion around how progressive librarians should prioritize workers and peasants reminds me of the semi-feudal and semi-colonial condition of the Philippines).

The key point to note is that government policies do not take into account the information needs of workers and peasants. This follows from the assumption on the part of planners, decision-makers and power-holders that there are no classes in their societies and that there are no specific needs that relate to specific classes. This assumption is based on the class interests of those in power and even if they are aware of different needs in different classes, they ignore the needs of workers and peasants for ideological reasons in their own class interest. Combined with that is the fact that capitalism and imperialism have taken power from workers and peasants and empowered the comprador class who are then programmed to meet the needs of capital, local and international.

In view of this, the question of power and power relations in these societies becomes crucial. This applies in the wider social areas of economic, political and cultural spheres as well as in specific sectors like libraries and information. This explains the reality of the situation for workers and peasants: they do not have power to formulate or implement policies; they do not have the power to change the direction of national policies from the market-orientated approach towards a socialist approach with equality and justice as key requirements; they do not control national resources to formulate policies; they do not have the infrastructure to

implement policies that are in their interest; they do not control educational institutions that train library and information workers whose training and skills are programmed to maintaining the status quo.

Given this situation, progressive organisations like PALIAct need to be clear about their role in meeting the needs of workers and peasants. First, they need to understand that the traditional libraries, their organisations and government policies will not change themselves to a people-orientated service. While the long-term goal is to move these national institutions to change their policies, in the short term some action can be taken. Some aspects of such action are:

1. People: For progressive social change to happen it needs progressive people: librarians, community workers, workers and peasants and their organisations, development workers, artists, progressive students and academics, among others. They will be the engine that brings about change.
2. Leadership: This will emerge from among the group of people mentioned above. They would not be afraid to learn from history and experiences from other countries.
3. Vision: develop a vision that can guide the new movement towards a people-oriented service with justice and equality in command.
4. Organisation: set up a progressive library organisation that can formulate alternative policies to provide relevant library and information services and also seek ways of influencing government policies. The organisation needs to bring together all progressive individuals and institutions that can work together.

An important requirement in achieving the above is resources. As there is no official backing for the initiative, there will not be funds to set up the organisation. In this situation, there is a need for self-reliance and those committed to change need to provide whatever resources they can and contribute in terms of their time and skills. This means that they need to be employed elsewhere for survival but to put in time and efforts in the new initiative as their contribution for change. Thus the initiative is not for people who seek gain such as employment or favours or services in return for work. The key requirement for the new organisation is commitment to equality and justice and enthusiasm to achieve meaningful change. While funds can be sought at a later stage when the organisation is strong, such external funds need to be rejected if they come with strings that subvert the vision of the organisation. There is boundless energy and commitment among workers and peasants and they will support this move if the aims and visions are clearly explained to them. It may be necessary for all those involved in the new initiative to attend study classes where they would learn about classes and class struggles, their own history, the politics of information etc so as to ensure they are committed to the new approach. Capitalism and imperialism have kept us ignorant about alternative information, ideas and experiences and the start of any movement for change needs to fill these gaps.

It is well to keep in mind that in the case of Mau Mau in Kenya, they did not wait for money from donor agencies to help them set up the resistance that ended colonialism. They used their own labour and resources, ideas and imagination to face a challenging enemy. That is the approach needed in the information world today.

4. After reading the article you co-authored Elizabeth Smallwood in the Progressive Librarian, what are the challenges that you've faced in international librarianship settings in combatting the idea of "neutrality" as a quality that the profession as a whole should strive towards?

The question of neutrality hides the larger political issues that are the background to the debate. Those who promote neutrality are in effect stating that they favour the status quo in a capitalist society. Being neutral means pretending not to take sides, which, in effect, means, supporting the power relations as they are. If the desire is to change the system so that those marginalised become the masters of their own destiny, then one cannot sit on the neutrality fence. One has to be on the side of those struggling to get their share of power and resources. In essence, key question are about class struggle and on whose side one stands.

The challenges we face are hidden and below-the-surface and so more difficult to identify and challenge. Nobody comes and says they are neutral or explains what neutrality means. They "show" themselves in the actions and results they achieve through their policies and practices. Here are some examples of how "neutrality" hits working people: when funds are taken away from services needed by working classes and given to the rich elite; when libraries are cut while the military keeps getting more funds; when hospitals, education and other services that benefit working people the most are reduced to fund taxes cuts for the rich; when library funds are used for travel and luxury books but not for books that support people's learning, awareness of their rights and exposure to experiences of resistance and change; when professional library staff are replaced by volunteers. All these policy decisions are made by politicians claiming to be neutral in allocating national resources.

So how does one challenge such "neutrality"? That is the key challenge in national as well as international context. It is necessary to challenge not only local library associations but international ones such as IFLA to ensure that such "neutrality" is exposed at all levels. At the same time politicians who claim to represent their constituents need to be effectively challenged, as do the corporations which squeeze out surplus from the labour of working people. In short, a social revolution is the only answer.

Librarians can bring about change in libraries by becoming active in the political sphere. They also need to redefine the social role of libraries under capitalism. But again, this cannot be achieved fully unless there is an internationalist approach. Working with other progressive people in many countries is more likely to change the mind-sets among police makers than just working on the level of individual countries.

Endnotes

1 Alfred Kagan (2015): Progressive Library Organizations: A Worldwide History. Jefferson NC, USA: McFarland. See also: Kagan, Al (2018): Progressive Library Organizations Update, 2013. Journal of Radical Librarianship, Vol. 4 (2018) pp.20–52. Available at: https://journal.radicallibrarianship.org/index.php/journal/article/view/27/38. [Accessed: 07-12-18].

2. In reflection of the imperial history of the country, the LA did not feel the need to use the term "British" before its name.

3 The Chartered Institute of Library and Information Professionals.

4 Durrani, Shiraz (2014): Progressive Librarianship: perspectives from Kenya and Britain, 1979-2010. Nairobi: Vita Books.

5 Durrani, Shiraz ((2008): Information and Liberation: writing on the politics of information and librarianship. Nairobi: Vita Books.

6 Details about this and other Projects mentioned are available in the two books quoted earlier.

ADDITIONAL READING

Copyright as a colonizer's tool—lessons from the 2018 #ccsummit Reflecting on learnings from the 2018 Creative Commons Global Summit in Toronto, Canada

I was happy to hear Chris Bourg remind us that "libraries have never been merely neutral repositories of knowledge" in her keynote at this weekend's Creative Commons Global Summit in Toronto. She elaborated that particularly in Western countries of the "global north", libraries were born out of colonialism, institutional oppression, and capitalism; academic libraries, in particular, have long been steeped in neoliberal ideology.

I think this statement is worth taking some time to unpack. Librarians of colour such as Fobazi Ettarh, have written about the institutional racism entrenched in library history. Ettarh highlights, for instance, the fact that millions of Black Americans were prohibited from public libraries in southern states before the civil rights movement. And in his paper, Trippin' Over the Color Line: The Invisibility of Race in Library and Information Studies , Todd Honma outlines the role the early public library played in promoting assimilation into the [white] mainstream and "Americanization" of immigrants as part of its mission. Just a couple weeks ago, Nicola Andrews shared her thoughtful and personal article on how libraries continue to uphold colonialism and white supremacy.

This idea that libraries–and by extension, the open access and open knowledge movements—are not neutral, nor inherently good, was a theme that I found myself revisiting throughout the summit.
The session opened with Kim Christen and Jane Anderson, who highlighted how archival practices often contribute to, and maintain, the colonial agenda. Large amounts of Indigenous knowledge and cultural materials (e.g. photographs, recordings) were extracted and archived by Western researchers over the last century; and although there are efforts to return these materials back to Indigenous communities, for the most part, Indigenous people—even those appearing in photographs— have no legal rights to these materials. Colonialism extends to metadata practices, too: a photo in an online collection often provides attribution to the photographer, but rarely the Indigenous subject in the photograph.
…
The session closed with Paul Williams, a lawyer

from Six Nations of the Grand River Territory. Williams spoke of the exploitative and extractive nature of ethnographers who transcribe sacred stories from Indigenous communities and then claim copyrights to those stories. Even more problematic? The fact that the original storyteller is often legally unable to access those transcriptions. He emphasized that for many Indigenous materials, the idea of public access is not appropriate. A settler applying an open license to an Indigenous cultural product should not decide that this product now belongs to the commons—or as Williams so succinctly put it, "Planting your flag in our garden doesn't make it your garden".

As a woman of colour and child of immigrants, I am guilty of brushing aside the privilege and problematic assumptions I hold as a settler. Although I have written about, and participated in, critiques of the lack of diversity in the Open Access communities, I have often failed to fully consider Indigenous perspectives. As such, this session was a necessary lesson to me that like libraries, and like the open information movement, copyright is not neutral. Copyright can be used as a tool for exerting control and ownership—and so quite fittingly, also as a tool for colonial practices. It was a reminder to me of the necessity of continuing to constantly interrogate our assumptions about what is good or useful, and to question who is not at the table.

Apr 18, 2018
Available at: https://medium.com/@lorraine_chu3n/copyright-as-
a-colonizers-tool-lessons-from-the-2018-ccsummit-7677963d798a
[Accessed: 15-05-19).

British fear of socialism

The British post-colonial policy in Kenya to relinquish formal political control while retaining immense influence through cultural, trade, economic and more so the military links literally came in to play during the independence talks…. Behind these manoeuvres by Britain though, there were fears that post- independence Kenya would be a socialist leaning country unless great effort was made to win over the politicians to support the Western capitalist ideology - Munene, Njagi Arthur (2013): The Colonial Legacy in Kenya-British Military Relations, 1963-2005. MA thesis, Kenyatta University.

VITA BOOKS

LIST OF BOOKS & PRICES (VAT EXCLUSIVE)

Pio Gama Pinto Kenya's Unsung Martyr. 1927 - 1965 edited by Shiraz Durrani 2018 ISBN 9789966189004 Pages 391 Kshs. 2,000.00/=	Mau Mau the Revolutionary, Anti-Imperialist Force from Kenya: 1948-1963 by Shiraz Durrani 2018 ISBN 9789966804020 Pages 154 Kshs. 800/=	Trade Unions in Kenya's War of Independence by Shiraz Durrani 2018 ISBN 9789966189097 Pages 118 Kshs. 800.00/=	People's Resistance to Colonialism and Imperialism in Kenya by Shiraz Durrani 2018 ISBN 9789966114525 Pages 124 Kshs. 800.00/=
Kenya's War of Independence: Mau Mau and its Legacy of Resistance to Colonialism and Imperialism, 1948-1990 by Shiraz Durrani 2018 ISBN 9789966189011 Pages 450 Kshs. 1,500.00/=	Liberating Minds, Restoring Kenyan History - Anti-Imperialist Resistance by Progressive South Asian Kenyans 1884-1965 by Nazmi Durrani 2017 ISBN 9789966189097 Pages 202 Kshs. 800.00/=	Makhan Singh. A Revolutionary Kenyan Trade Unionist Edited by Shiraz Durrani 2015 ISBN 1 86988613 5 Pages 194 Kshs. 1,200.00/=	Progressive Librarianship Perspectives from Kenya and Britain, 1979-2010 by Shiraz Durrani 2014 ISBN 9781869886202 Pages 446 Kshs. 1,700.00/=

Information and Liberation- Writings on the Politics of Information and Librarianship by Shiraz Durrani  2008 ISBN 9789966189073 Pages 384 Kshs. 1,700.00/=	Never be Silent - Publishing and Imperialism 1884-1963 by Shiraz Durrani  **2006** ISBN 9789966189073 Pages 280 Kshs. 1,000.00/=	Vita Books are available in Kenya from the following Bookshops: Bookstop Ltd, Yaya Centre, 2nd floor, Argwings Kodhek Road, P.O. Box 76203-00200, Nairobi. Chania Bookshop Ltd, Tumaini House, Ground floor, Moi Avenue, P.O. Box 32413, Nairobi. Prestige Bookshop, Prudential Building, Ground Floor - next to Imax, Mama Ngina Street, P.O. Box 67815-00200, Nairobi.

Forthcoming Publications from Vita Books
Tunakataa! We Say No! Poems of Resistance. By Nazmi Durrani

The poems depict peasant and worker resistance in Kenya in the 1980s to the oppressive Moi-KANU government. Here is the voice of people saying 'no' to capitalism and imperialism. The poems, in Kiswahili and English, are as relevant today as they were in the 1980s. They are as relevant in Kenya as they are in the rest of Africa struggling against capitalism and imperialism.

Two Paths Ahead: The Ideological Struggle for the Liberation of Kenya, 1960-1990. By Shiraz Durrani

The battles between socialism and capitalism in Kenya have been long, bitter and violent. Capitalism won with the active support of USA and UK governments at the time of independence in 1963. Yet the original Kenya African National Union (KANU) Party was in favour of socialism. It was Presidents Jomo Kenyatta and Daniel wrap Moi who used violence to suppress socialism and assassinated, disappeared, exiled or imprisoned its adherents. Capitalism became the unstated state policy. However, the desire for socialism never died. Resistance movements and opposition parties made socialism their aim, reflecting people's desire for justice, equality and empowerment.

Many studies on Kenya focus on personalities or 'tribes' or race, ignoring the all-important class and ideological position of organisations and their leaders. *Two Paths Ahead* examines the Kenyatta and Moi governments' support for capitalism and contrasts it with the socialist stand of the original KANU Party, the Kenya People's Union (KPU), the December Twelve Movement-Mwakenya as well as the voice of the 1982 coup leaders. This long history of socialism has also been suppressed by forces of capitalism represented by all the Kenyan governments since independence.

This book traces the battles between the two ideologies, between the radicals and the conservatives within and outside KANU. It looks at the struggle at the Lumumba Institute in the 1960s. It examines the position on land, social policy and worker rights through documents and actions of the opposing sides. It traces the stand of key leaders as proponents of either capitalism or socialism. The final section reproduces some of the documents which inform discussions on the ideological struggle in Kenya. The book exposes the hidden hand of imperialism in the country's rush to capitalism. It fills a gap in understanding the real contradictions that divide Kenya to this day.

Crimes of Capitalism in Kenya: Massacres, Murders, Detention, Imprisonment, Dissappearing and Exiling
Press cuttings on Moi's-KANU's Reign of Terror in Kenya, 1980s,
Research & Documentation Series No. 1 (2019)

Prepared from material in the Ukombozi Library
Much is written about the appalling human rights record of Presidents Jomo Kenyatta and Daniel arap Moi. However, these crimes are not attributed to the ideology that drove them: capitalism. The press cuttings in the first R&D Series records the brutal methods that KANU and imperialism used to remain in power. A future issue will focus on resistance to capitalism and the search for socialism.

P.O. Box 62501-00200
Nairobi. Kenya
http://vitabooks.co.uk
info.vitabkske@gmail.com
Distributed Worldwide in print
and eBooks by:
African Books Collective
www.africanbookscollective.com

Printed in the United States
By Bookmasters